PR
2831
C6

10853

Cole, ed.
    Twentieth century interpretations
of Romeo and Juliet

California Maritime Academy
Vallejo, California

1. All pupils in the school are entitled to use the library and to draw books.
2. Reference books, such as encyclopedias and dictionaries, are to be used only in the library.
3. Reserved books may be borrowed for one period, or at the close of school, and should be returned before the first class the following school day.
4. All other books may be retained for two weeks.
5. Two cents a day is charged for each book kept overtime.
6. Injury to books beyond reasonable wear and all losses shall be paid for.
7. No books may be taken from the library without being charged.

TWENTIETH CENTURY INTERPRETATIONS

OF

ROMEO AND JULIET

TWENTIETH CENTURY INTERPRETATIONS
OF

ROMEO AND JULIET

A Collection of Critical Essays

Edited by
DOUGLAS COLE

Prentice-Hall, Inc. *Englewood Cliffs, N. J.*
A SPECTRUM BOOK

PRENTICE-HALL INTERNATIONAL, INC. (*London*)
PRENTICE-HALL OF AUSTRALIA, PTY. LTD. (*Sydney*)
PRENTICE-HALL OF CANADA, LTD. (*Toronto*)
PRENTICE-HALL OF INDIA PRIVATE LIMITED (*New Delhi*)
PRENTICE-HALL OF JAPAN, INC. (*Tokyo*)

Contents

TWENTIETH CENTURY INTERPRETATIONS
OF
ROMEO AND JULIET

Introduction

by Douglas Cole

How does one create an enduring literary myth out of a sentimental romance, a love story already rehearsed in prose and verse in several languages? How does one turn a pair of young lovers into figures of such imaginative stature that they will fire the emotions of audiences for centuries to come and even obscure the competing images of lovers from classical mythology and medieval legend? Shakespeare never had to ask such questions of himself when he began to write *Romeo and Juliet*, but the response of the world audience to his play since that time has made them inevitable. No case has to be made for the continuing vitality of *Romeo and Juliet*. Its stage history (outmatched only by *Hamlet*'s) reveals a nearly unbroken chain of performances for more than three and a half centuries. It has inspired music, opera, ballet, literature, musical comedy, and film. Modern criticism, taking the play's impact for granted, attempts to elucidate some of the things that made Shakespeare's achievement possible (his source materials, his era's literary and dramatic conventions, and his own earlier writing, for example); to define the qualities of its structure and language; and to explore its relationships to Shakespeare's later tragedies. The results of this critical effort help us understand some of the answers to our opening questions, but not yet all.

Biographical Context

1595 is the date usually assigned to the writing of *Romeo and Juliet*. By this time William Shakespeare was thirty-one years old, had been married for twelve years, and was the father of three children. His extraordinary theatrical career was already on its way to both artistic and material success. He had been acting in London for the past five years, and early in that period had turned to playwriting as well. Most of his plays written before *Romeo and Juliet* were either histories or

1

comedies: the three parts of *Henry VI, Richard III, The Comedy of Errors, Love's Labour's Lost, The Taming of the Shrew, The Two Gentlemen of Verona.* Shakespeare would go on shortly to greater achievements in both these genres. *Richard II* and *Midsummer Night's Dream* appear to have been composed at nearly the same time as *Romeo and Juliet,* and just ahead lay the two parts of *Henry IV, Henry V,* and the romantic comedies, including *The Merchant of Venice, As You Like It,* and *Twelfth Night.* Later, at the turn of the century, Shakespeare would begin, with *Hamlet,* his unparalleled sequence of major tragedies: *Othello, King Lear, Macbeth, Antony and Cleopatra, Coriolanus.* Before *Romeo and Juliet* he had experimented with a tragedy in the Senecan vein, *Titus Andronicus; Julius Caesar* is placed after *Romeo and Juliet* and before *Hamlet.*

Meanwhile, Shakespeare had extended his theatrical interests by becoming in 1594 a principal shareholder in the acting company that was soon to be Elizabethan England's greatest success, the Lord Chamberlain's Men (known after the accession of King James as the "King's Men"). For this group and the theaters they came to own—the Globe and the Blackfriars—Shakespeare wrote almost all of his thirty-seven plays. Shakespeare prospered with the company, and was able to retire comfortably in 1611, when he rejoined his family at Stratford-upon-Avon. Seven years after his death in 1616, his fellow members of the King's Men were instrumental in publishing one of the finest treasures in world literature, the First Folio edition of Shakespeare's plays.

Of Shakespeare's non-dramatic poetry, the sonnets (154 in number) are best known. They are thought to have been written in the period 1592–1595, when the vogue of this poetic form was at its height in Elizabethan England. Two long narrative poems in the erotic tradition were also published during this time: *Venus and Adonis* and *The Rape of Lucrece.* Thus, in the years immediately preceding *Romeo and Juliet,* Shakespeare experimented not only with traditional poetic forms and conventions, but also with a wide range of attitudes and themes encompassing varieties of lust, love, and friendship. Such concerns find fresh expression in *Romeo and Juliet,* where they meet at the crossroads with tragedy.

Transformation of Sources and Conventions

It was common dramatic practice in Shakespeare's day to draw upon known history, legend, and story for the plot material of plays. Shakespeare did not have to invent the basic story of Romeo and Juliet. Nor did he have to invent a totally new kind of poetic language for handling the theme of love. Such a language lay at hand in contemporary love poetry, with its stock of characteristic metaphors, paradoxes, and conceits derived from Petrarch's famed Italian love poems. Neither was the combination of a lyrically developed love story and dramatic tragedy altogether novel, although it was far more common in the early Elizabethan theater to find love themes treated in comedy. Whatever hints were provided for Shakespeare by all these traditions he was able to refashion into something uniquely superior. Our own appreciation of that achievement can be enhanced by some exposure to the raw materials with which he worked.

The story of Romeo and Juliet was already an old one when Shakespeare decided to dramatize it for the Elizabethan stage. There were at least half a dozen versions circulating earlier in the century in Italy and France, and two of them had been adapted by English translators. Shakespeare apparently relied chiefly on Arthur Brooke's long poetic version, *The Tragical History of Romeus and Juliet,* first published in 1562 and reissued twenty-five years later. Some indication of how great a transformation Shakespeare effected can be glimpsed in the central speech of Brooke's Romeus in the scene corresponding to the play's balcony scene:

> Fair lady mine, dame Juliet, my life (quoth he)
> Even from my birth committed was to fatal sisters three.
> They may in spite of foes, draw forth my lively thread,
> And they also, who so saith nay, asunder may it shred.
> But who to reave my life, his rage and force would bend,
> Perhaps should try unto his pain how I it could defend.
> Ne yet I love it so, but always, for your sake,
> A sacrifice to death I would my wounded corpse betake.
> If my mishap were such, that here, before your sight,
> I should restore again to death, of life my borrowed light,
> This one thing and no more my parting sprite would rue:
> That part he should, before that you by certain trial knew
> The love I owe to you, the thrall I languish in,
> And how I dread to lose the gain which I do hope to win
> And how I wish for life, not for my proper ease,
> But that in it, you might I love, you honor, serve and please
> Till deadly pangs the sprite out of the corpse shall send.
> And thereupon he swore an oath, and so his tale had end.

Many modern readers of Shakespeare may be unaware of the immense difference between the ordinary verse of the Elizabethan age and Shakespearean poetry. They are likely to be even more unfamiliar with the usual quality of dramatic speech written for the developing Elizabethan stage. Only a few years before *Romeo and Juliet,* for instance, an early English love tragedy revised for the tastes of the 1590s offered this expression of a bereaved lover's grief (a young widow addresses her father):

> What hope of hap may cheer my hapless chance?
> What sighs, what tears may countervail my cares?
> What should I do, but still his death bewail,
> That was the solace of my life and soul?
> Now, now, I want the wonted guide and stay
> Of my desires and of my wreakless thoughts.
> My lord, my love, my life, my liking gone,
> In whom was all the fulness of my joy,
> To whom I gave the first-fruits of my love,
> Who with the comfort of his only sight
> All care and sorrows could from me remove.
> But, father, now my joys forepast to tell,
> Do but revive the horrors of my hell,
> As she that seems in darkness to behold
> The gladsome pleasures of the cheerful light.
>
> (Robert Wilmot, *Tancred and Gismund,* I. iii)

Shakespeare's achievement, of course, is not adequately measured by contrast with the poor dramatic poetry of his time. But we do well to remember that the passages cited above come from works presenting a combination of young lovers, tragic loss, and cruel destiny. These elements alone cannot ensure success, as Shakespeare himself demonstrated so comically in the Pyramus and Thisbe episode in *A Midsummer Night's Dream.*

The lyricism of Shakespeare's play lifts it far above the stumbling verse of other Elizabethan playwrights, and places it closer to the more literary traditions of love poetry, especially to the flourishing cult of the sonnet. The verse in *Romeo and Juliet* borrows heavily from sonnet conventions of metaphor and feeling, but manages also, as critics never tire of pointing out, to move beyond the conventions to something still more impressive. When Romeo and Juliet at their first encounter share the lines of a sonnet, Shakespeare shows us how a poetic convention can take on entirely new life in a dramatic context.

There is new life as well in Shakespeare's approach to the subject of young love itself. When the Elizabethans wrote tragedies of love, they were likely to emphasize the more lustful and obsessive qualities of passion, aspects which Shakespeare also had taken up in his long poems *Venus and Adonis* (1593) and *The Rape of Lucrece* (1594). The fashion in Italian tragedy, imitated both in France and in England, was to stress the mastery of the god Cupid, who was often portrayed as a malevolent, gloating tyrant. Some of this feeling filters into *Dido, Queen of Carthage,* the love tragedy written by Shakespeare's influential contemporary Christopher Marlowe. In *Dido* the heroine is more a victim than a celebrant of love, and the pattern of action stresses frustration and the pains of love denied or abandoned. The predominant strategy of Elizabethan dramatists was to present characters who were "love-crossed" rather than star-crossed. Their figures lack the sense of mutual dedication and individual purpose that inspires Romeo and Juliet. The love of Shakespeare's characters is conveyed with more compassion and innocence than can be found anywhere else in Renaissance drama.

Although Shakespeare's lovers are more idealized than those found either in Brooke's poem or in Elizabethan love tragedies, and although they speak with a language more lyrical than that of their counterparts in these earlier works, they never become ethereal fantasies. One major reason for this (and another distinguishing element in *Romeo and Juliet*) is the way in which passion and sentiment are modulated with both comic gusto and tragic irony. Mercutio and Juliet's Nurse, for example, are original comic developments of characters mentioned in the source story; in the play they not only become vital and amusing in themselves but also help to link the romance of Romeo and Juliet with an earthy sense of reality. On the tragic side, Shakespeare establishes thematic patterns of greater subtlety and paradox than the usual irony of "destructive passion"; his patterns suggest that even the virtues of loyalty, peace-making, and total personal dedication can unwittingly cooperate to bring about disaster.

Perhaps even more important is the way Shakespeare uses both comedy and tragedy to enhance each other in one play. His earlier *Titus Andronicus* had relied all too heavily on the sensationalistic devices of the neo-Senecan fashion in tragedy: wholesale slaughter, severed hands, rape, children's bodies cut up and served as part of their parents' meal. In *Romeo and Juliet,* thankfully, Shakespeare was trying something new. The tragic pattern he employed was imposed on materials, characters, and moods appropriate to comedy and romance: a comic nurse and clown, obstructing parents, duels of wit and parodic banter, the playful humor of hero and heroine. Shakespeare seems characteristically intent on stretching the range of tone usually assumed in early tragedy. He gives us not a comic play that somehow turns out tragically, but a more complex experience that weaves together intense, lyrically celebrated young love, vivacious and often bawdy wit, and the threatening, obstructive forces of ignorance, ill will, and chance—a combination which expresses the human impulse to affirm what is precious and beautiful in life in the very midst of a more pervasive hostility and baseness in the conditions and circumstances of life itself.

When compared with Shakespeare's later tragedies, the play may reveal a certain lack of profundity, a less far-reaching and momentous drive to open up the disturbing depths of human conduct and capacity. For some critics *Romeo and Juliet* is not yet "mature" tragedy; but we must remember that their norm is based on what Shakespeare himself did afterwards, not on what anyone in the Elizabethan theater had done earlier. It is perhaps fairer to say that the kind of tragic experience *Romeo and Juliet* offers us is different rather than immature, an experience less morally complex than others, but no less valid as an image of deeply moving aspects of our own awareness of life's promises and betrayals.

Poetic and Dramatic Language

If *Romeo and Juliet* marks Shakespeare's first original movement toward serious tragedy, it also marks a movement toward a dramatic language of increasing flexibility and expressiveness. The play shows the poet trying to integrate his skills of verse structure, rhyme, metaphor, and ingenious word-play with dramatic skills of characterization through style of language and gesture, exposition through action as well as declamation, and imagery patterns that function to bind a diversified scenario into a unified thematic order. Shakespeare's work here displays a texture of marked formality, notable in the abundant rhyme, extended conceits, and above all in a wide range of "set pieces" —among them Mercutio's Queen Mab passage, Friar Lawrence's sermons, Juliet's epithalamion, Paris's elegy, the sonnet shared by the lovers at their first meeting, and the *aubade* at their farewell. In patterning so much of the dialogue on these very literary models, Shakespeare was clearly stretching his medium to see what it could do. He was writing this play in the period that included the highly elaborated language of *Love's Labour's Lost,* the extended complaints of *Richard II,* the lavishly decorative erotic poems *Venus and Adonis* and *The Rape of Lucrece,* and his own contribution to the sonnet-cycle fashion.

In *Romeo and Juliet* we find Shakespeare's virtuosity with formal poetic language extended not only by the demands of dramatic context, but also by an awareness of how easily formality may slip into artificiality. Shakespeare seems to have delighted in trying his hand at many different kinds of verbal play, but always with some tact about crossing the boundaries of what is truly acceptable. More than any other dramatist of the period, he is capable of inserting near-parodies of the conventional themes and devices he is exploiting. By such means he seems to remind his audience, as Juliet reminds Romeo: "Conceit [i.e., true understanding or invention], more rich in matter than in words,/Brags of his substance, not of ornament."

Coleridge was perhaps right when he claimed that in this play the poet had not yet "entirely blended" with the dramatist, implying that these elements of poetic formality do not always seem to work effectively in dramatic context. Samuel Johnson much earlier had complained that the characters were always left with a conceit [i.e., an elaborate parallel or metaphor] in their misery—"a miserable conceit"; and actors and actresses in every generation have had their problems with the labored lamentations of Juliet and Romeo in Act Three. Critics move from such examples of awkwardness (only awkwardly justified by the Elizabethan taste for that sort of thing), to matters of tired convention or excessively developed imagery, such as we find in Romeo's first speeches on love or Lady Capulet's comparison of Paris to a book. Here there is more room for argument that Shakespeare knew what he was doing in supplying the love-sick pup Romeo with the most familiar catalogue of Petrarchan oxymora ("O brawling love, O loving hate, . . . O heavy lightness, serious vanity, . . . Feather of lead, bright smoke, cold fire, sick health. . . ."), or giving Lady Capulet such artificially toned sentiments, or providing such a bathetic chorus of grief in the Capulet household when Juliet's "death" is discovered. One can sense in the kind of language used at such points a corresponding emotional or imaginative immaturity in the character, a weakness which will help define later a strength or intensity somewhere else. In a play that works so well with contrasts in theme and mood, contrasts in language have a fit place.

Most critical skepticism disappears in response to the lyrical language of the balcony scene or of the farewell at dawn. Many playgoers know the purple passages from these scenes by heart, but what is often forgotten is the way Shakespeare has rendered his poetry effective by constructing the scene which contains it so that theatrical dimensions (setting, timing, entrances and exits, interplay between characters, etc.) provide the real foundation for the charm and power of the words.

There is a "language" in the scenario itself, and in the sequence of
actions and reactions within a given scene, which enables the poetic
language to convey its maximum meaning and feeling. A brief analysis
of the balcony scene will suggest how this happens.

Shakespeare turned from a neat and symmetrical exchange of
speeches in Brooke's poem to construct an entirely new thing, filled
with surprises, artful changes of pace, dramatic interruptions, warm
humor, and a delightful interplay between the fragile puff paste of
lovers' poetry and the strong, actual feelings beneath it. The balcony
scene "works" not so much because of its rich sentiment (though
theatrical interpreters of previous ages have frequently done much to
intensify its sentimentality) but because that sentiment is poised with
such masterful balance in a dramatic configuration. The emotional
richness of the scene is partly a product of the lovers' feelings, and
partly of the way Shakespeare makes us relate those feelings to the
play's earlier atmosphere, which has been largely comic, and to the
already predicted tragedy to come. The first relationship is stressed by
the scene's irreverent preface: Mercutio's bawdy "conjuring" of the
Romeo love-sick for Rosaline. Mercutio's mocking parody of love
equates it with sex; his is an earthy, recognizable, and totally anti-
sentimental attitude. Shakespeare gives it stage-center attention, and
then, with astonishing abruptness, shifts to the central exchange between his lovers. Mercutio's barbs are deflected because they are cast
at the wrong target, because they are part of his role as entertainer,
and because the attitudes of the lovers as they are developed in the
following scene include but transcend the physical realities of love.

Romeo's imagery, still somewhat conventional in the way of lover's
rhetoric, is the first means by which Mercutio's earth is left below:
his twenty-five lines of praise for Juliet center on a sequence of conceits using sun, moon, stars, and angels as their bases. By this time we
have come to expect such things of Romeo, but even so the register
has changed from the gentle satire on his earlier melancholy to a more
firmly romantic note. If there is any risk of responding to this scene
with too great a sense of its (or Romeo's) artificiality, Shakespeare
seems to counter it by shifting attention to Juliet, the girl experiencing
her first love and expressing it here without benefit of a practiced sonneteer's vocabulary. The first movement of the balcony scene, a movement in which each figure speaks in a kind of soliloquy, ends in Juliet's
"What's in a name" passage. Shakespeare moves that passage to its
perfect climax: "And for thy name, which is no part of thee, / Take
all myself." At this instant, moreover, he shows us the dramatist at
one with the poet: Juliet's speech ends in mid-line; its offer cannot be

ignored by the concealed Romeo, who steps out of hiding to finish the line with his echoing "I take thee at thy word."

Juliet's great surprise here begins the second movement of the scene; her flurry of questions—each quickly, anxiously, and realistically put —is met by poetizing comments on Love by Romeo, who discounts all danger in professing his dedication to her. The contrast between their styles of thought is capped by Juliet's first long speech directly to him (II. ii. 85–106), in which she confesses her own want of formality in disclosing the truth of her love. Though very young, she knows of lovers' perjuries; and in the following interchange concerning Romeo's vow of love to her, she has the charming triumph of managing to interrupt his vow in mid-breath with her perfect "Well, do not swear." The dramatic interchange between them has been enough to convince her of his love: the rhetoric, the conceits, the poetry are to Juliet somehow superfluous; and it is this feeling, made explicit by her sense of realism, which manages to transform all the love-worn phrases and promises into vital and convincing statements.

This second movement of the scene centers around the subject of Romeo's vow, but the pace and balance of the dialogue give Juliet the key part: she introduces each new theme and Romeo responds. One of his responses marks the transition to the scene's third movement (ll. 125–154): to Juliet's "goodnight" he replies "O wilt thou leave me so unsatisfied?"—and we are now centered on the subject of Juliet's vow to him. It has in fact already been given, she says, but adds its better echo:

> My bounty is as boundless as the sea,
> My love as deep; the more I give to thee,
> The more I have, for both are infinite.

How do you move beyond a line like that? Shakespeare doesn't close the scene there, but he interrupts it—with the calling voice of the Nurse. And here, by the simple element of intrusive noise, we are reminded of the outside world, the world of old people and hostile feuds, the world of threats and dangers that for the moment has been quite forgotten. The lyric mood, if you will, has been broken, but with a vital dramatic point; like Juliet's earlier premonition of fear at the suddenness of their love, the interruption reinvokes the outer pattern of tragedy that the play's prologue had initially established. The lovers are alone and not alone; first they discover each other and then they— and the audience—are made aware of what lies beyond. For Juliet at this point there is no great problem: she runs off for a moment, first bidding Romeo to await her return. When she comes back, she delivers a rapid-fire "three words"—amounting to arrangements on the morrow for setting up their marriage rites. All the while the Nurse calls and Juliet's attentions are drawn between her message for Romeo and the urgency to get back inside lest anything go wrong. "A thousand times goodnight!" she concludes, and neither Romeo nor we expect to see her again.

Romeo moves away for his exit, only to be stopped by the surprising third entrance of his beloved. Now in the fourth and final movement of the scene, devoted not to any subject but only to exhibit the reluctance of the lovers to part, we get a final glimpse of the mutuality of their affection, and the lack of any need for words or reasons to justify their delight in being together. Juliet once more delivers the key speech of the movement—centering in the delicately ironic image of the little bird she may kill with too much cherishing—and Romeo continues to respond to her metaphors rather than offer his own from a more second-hand stock. After the *final* goodnights, the ensuing scene presents us with the meditative Friar, discoursing on the ambiguity of nature's treasures, beauty and poison, fragrance and death, vitality and corruption. Leaving Mercutio's earthiness far behind during the balcony scene, we are moved now into another kind of remembrance of earth and of the duality and precarious balance of natural things.

In between, we have heard poetry and watched a carefully varied action evoke the beauty of young people in love, subtly punctuated with hints of danger, intrusion, and fear. The scene's combination of the lyrical mutuality of the lovers with the felt (and heard) presence of the interrupting outside world corresponds to the central tragic plight of the love story. A similar combination will occur in the equally memorable leave-taking scene (III. v), and has already occurred in the lovers' first meeting at the ball, when the fuming of Tybalt and the bustling of Capulet provide the threatening, intrusive image, held in counterpoint with the shared sonnet of the lovers. Shakespeare does not allow his lyricism to exist in a static context; he puts it "on stage" in contexts which embody in sight and sound the precarious and tragic balance of life's joys as they are envisioned in the play as a whole.

Structure

Critical commonplaces regarding the structure of *Romeo and Juliet* tend to emphasize a handful of its characteristics: the swift pace of the action, which Shakespeare compresses into a few days' duration dramatized in two dozen scenes, many of which center on sudden reversals and the need for quick decisions; the emphatic juxtaposition of comic characters and attitudes with foreboding and destructive situations; the heightening of the young lovers' purity of feeling by contrast both with the lustier attitudes of the Nurse and Mercutio and with Romeo's studied infatuation with Rosaline; the more obvious contrasts between love and hate, youth and age, impetuous action and helpless wisdom; the efficiency and impact of the central reversal scene of Mercutio's death; and finally, for critics with allegiance to Aristotelian tragic formulas, the excessive reliance on sheer accident or chance in order to move the events toward a disaster which seems less inevitable than tragedy demands.

Qualities of pace and contrast are best sensed in performance, where it becomes clear how increasingly masterful Shakespeare's theatrical skill is becoming. He is able to convey more by the pace and proportion of action than he had been even in the violent early history plays. "Proportion" is perhaps a vague term, but it does cover the skill by which Shakespeare shapes his presentation of the lovers' destiny. We are never *directly* aware, for example, that Romeo and Juliet are actually together to share only 330 lines throughout the whole play, about one-ninth of the play's length; but that proportion helps nevertheless to accent the intensity and rarity of feeling embodied in their encounters, as well as to impress upon us the weight and complexity of the outside world's "doings" which obstruct the couple and aid in destroying them. More than half of those lines, moreover, are in the balcony scene. Shakespeare, elsewhere, has been incredibly sparing: some 18 lines in the ball scene (14 of those the shared sonnet); 10 in the Friar's cell just before the marriage; 66 at their dawn farewell; and 46 in the tomb. It is true that their thoughts about each other are expressed even when they are separated, but the rarity of their actual presence together on stage still makes its central point in a dynamic way.

The comic texture of the play is also kept under a fine control. Roughly one-sixth of the total dialogue can be called comic, and practically all of it is confined to that part of the play before Mercutio's death. It helps to build, even within the more threatening outlines of the family feud, a hearty atmosphere of comradeship, wit, gaiety and high spirits—an atmosphere which seems to hold out a promise for the budding love of Romeo and Juliet, but which turns out to be explosive. Each comic character or event is made to harbor an ironic counterthrust: the gaiety at the ball is marred by a vengeful Tybalt; the witty Mercutio harbors a fatal itch to fight; the sympathetic Nurse betrays her drastic lack of sensitivity when she urges Juliet to forget

Romeo and marry Paris. The unifying symbol for these comic people and events, as well as for the lovers themselves and the bustling world about them, can be found in the Friar's osier cage: those flowers, plants, and weeds—some beautiful, many capable of both healing and destroying, all very natural and part of the mortal earth.

> The earth that's nature's mother is her tomb;
> What is her burying grave, that is her womb;
> And from her womb children of divers kind
> We sucking on her natural bosom find:
> Many for many virtues excellent,
> None but for some, and yet all different.
> O mickle is the powerful grace that lies
> In plants, herbs, stones, and their true qualities;
> For nought so vile that on the earth doth live
> But to the earth some special good doth give;
> Nor aught so good but, strained from that fair use,
> Revolts from true birth, stumbling on abuse.
> Virtue itself turns vice, being misapplied,
> And vice sometime by action dignified.   [II. iii. 9–22]

That comedy and tragedy lie down together in this play not only points up the reversal in mood that takes place with the killing of Mercutio and Tybalt, but illustrates again the inner paradox of our mortal nature.

Theme

I take that paradox, as stated by the Friar, to be at the heart of this play, and also a foreshadowing of a theme given further embodiment in Shakespeare's later tragedies. Others have suggested differing central themes for *Romeo and Juliet,* ranging from a literal insistence on the lovers' star-crossed fate, to a Freudian view of their experience as an embodiment of the death-wish; from a neo-orthodox-Elizabethan lesson in the dangers of passion, to a providential triumph of love over hate.

The reasons for such diversity are discoverable in the play, which seems to hold out a number of keys to interpretation. If we look only at the conclusion, with the reconciled parents and the promise of a golden monument, we may be inclined to see the mysterious ways of Providence working toward good. If we listen chiefly to the Friar's moral admonitions, rather than to his reflections on the natural condition cited above, we may agree that haste and lack of wise forethought bring about the disaster. If we catalogue all the tricks played by chance (particularly Friar John's undelivered message and the unhappy timing of arrivals and awakenings in the final scene), we may see it all as the workings of a hostile external Fate. Tragic theorists become disheartened at the lack of a more highly developed moral consciousness in the central figures and the corresponding lack of close cause-and-effect integration between such characterization and the destructive outcome. And students of Elizabethan piety (both familial and religious) are inclined to feel more harshly about Romeo and Juliet themselves than even Friar Lawrence does at his most chiding moments. The interpretive problem is a problem involving proportion and balance; a balanced view of the play must rest on an awareness of the delicate balance of its diverse elements. To emphasize one to the exclusion of the rest will not give us a theme worthy of the play's actual structure or the dramatic experience it yields in performance.

It is undeniable that the strategy of the play generates strong sympathy for the lovers, heightens their superiority in richness and purity of feeling, and awakens our compassion for their plight. It is also undeniable that Romeo in particular is both reckless and desperate at the wrong moments; partly because he is in love, partly because he is young, partly because he is the histrionic Romeo. By the end of the play Shakespeare makes more of a man of him than the miserable boy (of Act III) grovelling in tears on the Friar's floor, but he also gives him a cruel power with that added strength and determination: the slaying of Paris is the dramatic proof. The combination is deliberate: Shakespeare's sources contain neither the heightened sense of the lovers' innocence nor Paris's murder. The play does not prove that Romeo and Juliet should not have yielded to their love for one another, or disobeyed their parents, or been so quick to marry or to kill themselves. It does suggest that the flower of an innocent love, because of the earth in which it was planted, could foster its own destruction. Shakespeare hints at a natural disaster rather than a moral one, but his conclusion urges something beyond disaster: that such a destruction may in turn foster the reconciliation of the elders who do not understand love. The beauty and harmony of the lovers does not die with them.

To view the combination or the paradox this way is to see the truth and wisdom of the Friar's first meditative speech, already quoted. We need not discount his spiritual sagacity in order to side with the lovers (though we may entertain some doubts about his pragmatic sense). In him Shakespeare seems to be providing a perspective which is in line with the character of a religious counsellor but also moves beyond into a more universal probing of forces at work in the natural world. The technique involved is somewhat similar to the famous gardener's scene in *Richard II* (III. iv), where an interpretive comment on the political problems of the play is embodied in the metaphor of gardening by very minor characters. The Friar is of course a more important and more integrated figure in the plot of *Romeo and Juliet,* and the kind of radial thematic utterance Shakespeare gives him is less allegorically imposed. Yet the function remains similar. In later plays, such radial statements and metaphysical "soundings" will be incorporated into the reflections of Shakespeare's tragic heroes. One of the reasons Romeo seems less complex and less interesting than these later figures is that he is not given such reflections or the kind of awareness that would prompt them. The nature of man (or of woman) is never the subject of his meditations or agonies; and even his comments on the nature of love are artificial and "literary" compared to the intensely vital commentary of his actions.

If even an innocent and idealized love can inspire recklessness, its opposites can do so with greater consequence. The unmotivated mutual hate of the feud, the stupidity of its violent expressions, are the very first impressions Shakespeare's dramatic action presents to us. There is a more subtle and less culpable variant of such passion in the eagerness of Mercutio, who is outside the family lines of battle, to get the best of the irksome Tybalt. His mercurial temperament is accentuated by the contrasting tolerance and good will of his and Romeo's friend Benvolio. Shakespeare does not mean to reduce them to counterparts of the Friar's "grace and rude will," but the impulse behind their pairing is surely connected with that duality.

The envy, ill will, and aggressiveness that characterize the feud do not represent the total threat to the love of the central figures. The feud is always present as a dangerous obstructing condition; it is a reason for keeping things secret which if known would resolve many complications. But it is not of itself a villainous thing that destroys the lovers intentionally. To understand its limitations as an element in the whole balance is to realize that the play cannot be summed up as a conflict between the forces of young love and old hate. Tragic destruction results from a pattern which includes as well the unaccountable element of chance and the more pervading element of unawareness. So many incidents in the play exhibit people who do not know what they are really doing, people who are both agents and victims of an unthinking impetuosity. The spectrum ranges from the vulgar servants of the opening scene through Mercutio's duel, Capulet's marriage-planning, the murder of Paris, to Romeo's suicide and the Friar's fear of being discovered at the tomb. Clearly this kind of unawareness leads to an irony often associated with tragedy (although it is also a standard tool of the comedy writer who builds a complication out of interlocking misunderstandings), but in the context of Shakespeare's play it does more than heighten suspense and trigger an agonized "If only he knew!" audience reaction. It serves to impress upon us a basic condition of human interaction—our unconscious limitations in understanding the motives of others (and of ourselves), our ultimate helplessness in the face of the multiple possibilities of things going awry. Once this quality is fully felt, we cannot be content with condemning either stupidity or "rude will" as the basis of destructive evil. We are led once more to an insight or a perception of the mortal world which is broader than the strictly moral one: tragic destruction, though often the consequence of human decision, is beyond that an irremediable aspect of the natural world and man's limited consciousness. That perception is somewhat muted by Shakespeare's concluding reconciliation, but because it is grounded in the conditions of human interaction in the play, it cannot be an element totally "resolved" by this or any other kind of ending.

Fate and Coincidence

Two final problems related to this quality or insight remain. One is the problem of Fate. The other is the feeling that *Romeo and Juliet* lacks tragic inevitability precisely because so much of the action turns on ignorance that might have been remedied and on sheer mistiming. The prologue, the foreboding dreams and intimations of death, and the futility of the elaborately planned attempts to restore Romeo and Juliet to one another all tend to stress that the destiny of the lovers is fated. Each move that they make toward each other is matched by some counterthrust; and though there is no villain or human agent behind the opposition, some readers have felt that Fate itself takes on the quality of a destructive agent, moving events and characters in cruel combination to produce the disastrous outcome. Romeo may want to defy the stars, but in that very defiance he is unwittingly co-operating in his own doom. The trouble with this interpretation again lies in what it must leave out or ignore. If we are to judge the reconciling conclusion of the play as inappropriate to the major design of the tragedy, as a last-minute excrescence that does not fit well with earlier motifs, then perhaps we may rest content with the vision of inimical Fate. But if we see the ending as purposeful, and as an evocation of the paradoxical good that can spring from a lamented destruction, the simple view of Fate will not satisfy. Nor can we ignore what Shakespeare characteristically stresses in all his tragic drama: the connections between the character of men and the disaster that may befall them. In this case, we have only to recall the care Shakespeare has taken to show us Romeo in an unheroic and desperate hysteria after he has killed Tybalt: a scene frequently embarrassing to actors but nevertheless integral to the play. It shows us the emotional proclivity in Romeo without which the external misfortunes and mischances would not have culminated in his death. If Shakespeare had wanted to put full strength into the Fate motif, he could also have employed such allegorical devices as had appeared in the contemporary play *Soliman and Perseda,* in which choral figures called Love, Death, and Fortune debate the relative power of their influence on the human lives in the story. The personification of a hostile Fate or Fortune was a fashionable convention in the neo-Senecan tragedy of the Elizabethans; the theme was equally conventional. In *Romeo and Juliet,* however, Shakespeare was moving in another direction. His developing vision of a tragic universe was not to be defined by hostile fatality, but by a paradoxical and all too precarious balance of good and evil.

And what about Chance? If we do not interpret it as the tool of a hostile agency, we still have to accommodate its large role in the play. Does it deplete the sense of the tragic? For Aristotle, it would have, as it has for his followers. If every effect is to have a necessary cause, or if any drastic result must have some antecedents that render it probable, we will be especially discomfited by Friar John's inability to deliver the message to Romeo that would have saved both his and Juliet's life. I have always harbored the suspicion that such discomfiture is more a product of logical Aristotelianism than of the play. We can always revise the improbability in our imagination, but I doubt if we succeed in getting a more tragic effect. Let the message reach Romeo in time; let him rush to be present at the side of the waking Juliet; and let him meet the grieving Paris there, to be slain by Paris in the confusion of misunderstanding. We would lose much more than the occasion for some great poetry and intense pathos; we would lose the tragic connection between the value of love, the radiance and desperation of passion, and the combined joy and sorrow of man in the condition of time.

Time is the enemy even more than chance; it presses in upon the lovers in countless ways—the dawn brings the threat of discovery; a bare second enables the envious sword of Tybalt to fell Mercutio; the marriage date foreshortened by a capricious Capulet demands swift counterplans and decisions, which bring, in turn, disaster. The fast-paced world that Shakespeare builds up around his characters allows little possibility for adherence to Friar Lawrence's counsel of "Wisely and slow." In such a world to stumble tragically is surely no less inevitable than it is for Lear to go mad in the face of human ingratitude. In a vivid performance of the play, things happen so swiftly and suddenly that issues of probability hardly arise. Add the fact that the *emotions* behind the catastrophe have been made probable, and we readily see why we do not look upon the death of Romeo and Juliet as merely a terrible accident.

It is possible to step back from the immediate emotional grip of *Romeo and Juliet* and discover that we have somehow been taken in, that the swiftly moving world of sudden love and sudden death has been arbitrarily contrived, that the mechanism of the plot and the ingenious conceits of the language display a rather self-conscious artistry. At this second level of response, we may become aware that, for all its virtues, the play does not exhibit the power, range, and deeply probing qualities of *Hamlet, Othello, Macbeth* or *Lear*. Its reflective, philosophical dimensions are confined rather tightly to a few discourses by Friar Lawrence, where they remain detached from the emotional intensity of the chief characters; in *Hamlet* and *Lear* those who question the dignity of man and the nature of the gods are those who also suffer the greatest torments. *Romeo and Juliet* is surely a more honest expression of human tragedy than the grotesque *Titus Andronicus* or the melodramatic *Richard III,* but it has not yet found the most potent articulation for the paradox of good and evil in the natural world. If we feel finally that the play is not *major* tragedy, it is for such reasons rather than for defects in probability. A moving and compassionate expression of intense and vital passions, it burns with a flame more luminous than searing.

To a certain extent, it cannot do otherwise, granted its subject. As a close-up study of a breath-taking young love, it has little time or place for the probing inner conflicts of Shakespeare's more mature and deeply disillusioned characters. Indeed, one of the marks of the lovers' innocence is that they remain untouched by the experience of disillusionment, the experience that sounds the bass note of tragic anxiety from *Julius Caesar* on and echoes throughout Shakespeare's so-called "problem plays" and later romances as well. Romeo and Juliet are all in all to one another; the radiance of their shared love illumines them with glowing beauty, but casts little light on the world around them. Their experience, and ours as an audience, is thus intense but circumscribed. Shakespeare's structure of contrasts and paradoxes sets off that experience in a rich and colorful design, but he does not choose to emphasize in it the more disturbing deeper shadows that he was soon to explore with such comprehension. Here he was content to temper extremities with extreme sweet, and in view now of the world's reaction to his play who is to say he chose wrongly?

Romeo and Juliet—The Conduct of the Action

by Harley Granville-Barker

The dominating merit of this is that Shakespeare takes Brooke's tale, and at once doubles its dramatic value by turning its months to days.

> These violent delights have violent ends. . . .

and a sense of swiftness belongs to them, too. A Hamlet may wait and wait for his revenge; but it accords with this love and its tragedy that four days should see its birth, consummation and end. Incidentally we can here see the "Double Time"—which has so exercised the ingenuity of commentators, who will credit him with their own—slipping naturally and easily into existence.[1] He makes dramatic use of time when he needs to.

> *Capulet.* But soft, what day is this?
> *Paris.*   Monday, my lord.
> *Capulet.* Monday! Ha! ha! Well, Wednesday is too soon;
>   O' Thursday let it be:—o' Thursday, tell her,
>   She shall be married to this noble earl. . . .

This sense of the marriage looming but three days ahead is dramatically important; later to intensify it, he even lessens the interval by a day. But (his mind reverting now and then to Brooke's story as he read

---

From "Romeo and Juliet," in Prefaces to Shakespeare, Vol. II, by Harley Granville-Barker (Princeton: Princeton University Press, 1947; London: B. T. Batsford Ltd.) Copyright 1947 by Princeton University Press; illustrated edition copyright © 1963 by The Trustees of the Author; notes to the illustrations copyright © 1963 by M. St. Salre Byrnes. Reprinted by permission of the publishers.

[1] In the Preface to *The Merchant of Venice* this discussion is raised again, and, of course, pursued at length in *Othello.*

it, possibly before he saw that he must weave it closer) he will care-
lessly drop in phrases that are quite contradictory when we examine
them. But what audience will examine them as they flash by?

> I anger her sometimes [says the Nurse to Romeo], and tell her that
> Paris is the properer man. . . .

(when neither Paris nor Romeo has been in the field for four and
twenty hours).

> Is it more sin to wish me thus forsworn,
> Or to dispraise my lord with that same tongue
> Which she hath praised him with above compare
> So many thousand times?

(when, all allowance made for Juliet's exaggeration, the Nurse has
not had twice twenty-four hours in which to praise or dispraise). But
notice that this suggestion of the casual slackness of normal life con-
veniently loosens the tension of the tragedy a little. There is, indeed,
less of carelessness than a sort of instinctive artistry about it; and the
method is a natural by-product of the freedom of Shakespeare's theater.

But he marshals his main action to very definite purpose. He begins
it, not with the star-crossed lovers (though a prologue warns us of
them), but with a clash of the two houses; and there is far more significance in this than lies in the fighting. The servants, not the masters,
start the quarrel. If Tybalt is a firebrand, Benvolio is a peacemaker;
and though Montague and Capulet themselves are drawn in, they have
the grace to be a little ashamed after. The hate is cankered; it is an
ancient quarrel set new abroad; and even the tetchy Capulet owns
that it should not be so hard for men of their age to keep the peace. If
it were not for the servants, then, who fight because they always have
fought, and the Tybalts, who will quarrel about nothing sooner than
not quarrel at all, it is a feud ripe for settling; everyone is weary of
it; and no one more weary, more impatient with it than Romeo;

> O me! What fray was here?
> Yet tell me not—for I have heard it all. . . .

We are not launching, then, into a tragedy of fated disaster, but—
for a more poignant if less highly heroic theme—of opportunity muddled away and marred by ill-luck. As a man of affairs, poor Friar
Laurence proved deplorable; but he had imagination. Nothing was
likelier than that the Montagues and Capulets, waking one morning
to find Romeo and Juliet married, would have been only too thankful
for the excuse to stop killing each other.

> And the continuance of their parents' rage,
> Which, but their children's end, nought could remove . . .

says the Prologue. Nought in such a world as this, surmises the young Shakespeare; in a world where

> I thought all for the best.

avails a hero little; for on the heels of it comes

> O, I am fortune's fool!

Having stated his theme, he develops it, as his habit already is (and was to remain; the method so obviously suits the continuities of the Elizabethan stage), by episodes of immediate contrast in character and treatment. Thus, after the bracing rattle of the fight and the clarion of the Prince's judgment, we have our first sight of Romeo, fantastic, rueful, self-absorbed. His coming is preluded by a long passage of word-music; and, that its relevance may be plain, the verse slips into the tune of it at the first mention of his name. Benvolio's brisk story of the quarrel, dashed with irony, is finishing—

> While we were interchanging thrusts and blows,
> Came more and more, and fought on part and part,
> Till the Prince came, who parted either part.

—when Lady Montague interposes with

> O, where is Romeo? Saw you him to-day?
> Right glad am I he was not at this fray.

and promptly, like a change from wood-wind, brass and tympani to an andante on the strings, comes Benvolio's

> Madam, an hour before the worshipped sun
> Peered forth the golden window of the east . . .

Montague echoes him; and to the wooing smoothness of

> But he, his own affections' counsellor,
> Is to himself—I will not say how true—
> But to himself so secret and so close,
> So far from sounding and discovery,
> As is the bud bit with an envious worm,
> Ere he can spread his sweet leaves to the air,
> Or dedicate his beauty to the sun.
> Could we but learn from whence his sorrows grow,
> We would as willingly give cure as know.

Romeo appears; moody, oblivious of them all three. It is a piece of technique that belongs both to Shakespeare's stage in its simplicity and to the play's own lyrical cast.

Then (for contrasts of character and subject), close upon Romeo's mordant thought-play and word-play with Benvolio come Capulet and Paris, the sugary old tyrant and the man of wax, matchmaking—and such a good match for Juliet as it is to be! Close upon this comes Benvolio's wager that he'll show Romeo at the feast beauties to put Rosaline in the shade; and upon that, our first sight of Juliet, when she is bid take a liking to Paris at the feast if she can.

The scene of the procession of the Maskers to Capulet's house (with Romeo a spoil-sport as befits his mood) is unduly lengthened by the bravura of the Queen Mab speech, which is as much and as little to be dramatically justified as a song in an opera is.[2] But Shakespeare makes it serve to quicken the temper of the action to a pitch against which—as against the dance, too, and Tybalt's rage—Romeo's first encounter with Juliet will show with a quiet beauty all its own. Did he wonder for a moment how to make this stand out from everything else in the play? They share the speaking of a sonnet between them, and it is a charming device.

One must picture them there. The dance is over, the guests and the Maskers are in a little chattering, receding crowd, and the two find themselves alone.[3] Juliet would be for joining the others; but Romeo, his mask doffed, moves towards her, as a pilgrim towards a shrine.

> If I profane with my unworthiest hand . . .

It is hard to see what better first encounter could have been devised. To have lit mutual passion in them at once would have been common-place; the cheapest of love tragedies might begin like that. But there

[2] The young gentlemen are gate-crashers, we perceive; there are few novelties in the social world! But Capulet is delighted; he even, when the unlooked-for fun is over and the recalcitrant regular guests have been coaxed to dance, presses a "trifling foolish banquet" upon the strangers; cake and wine upon the sideboard, that is to say, and not, as the word now implies, a substantial sit-down affair. But etiquette, it seems, is against this. Having measured them a measure and so wound up the occasion very merrily, the "strangers" do begone. Seriously, the conduct of this scene, when it is staged, needs attention. It is generally quite mis-understood and misinterpreted.

[3] The company, that is to say, drift up towards the inner stage, from which, as from the withdrawing rooms beyond the great hall, Capulet and the guests had come to welcome the masked invasion, and as they all move away the guessing at who the strangers are dies down.

is something sacramental in this ceremony, something shy and grave and sweet; it is a marriage made already. And she is such a child; touched to earnestness by his trembling earnestness, but breaking into fun at last (her defense when the granted kiss lights passion in him) as the last quatrain's meter breaks for its ending into

> You kiss by the book.

The tragedy to come will be deepened when we remember the innocence of its beginning. The encounter's ending has significance too. They are not left to live in a fool's paradise for long. Romeo hears who she is and faces his fate. An hour ago he was affecting melancholy while Mercutio and his fellows laughed round him. Now, with the sport at its best, he braces to desperate reality. Then, as the guests and Maskers depart and the laughter dies, Juliet grows fearful. She hears her fate and must face it, too.

> My only love sprung from my only hate!
> Too early seen unknown, and known too late!
> Prodigious birth of love it is to me
> That I must love a loathed enemy.

The child is no more a child.

A chorus follows. This may have some further function than to fill up time while furniture is shifted or stage fittings are adjusted; it is of no dramatic use.[4] Then Romeo appears alone.

And now, with his finest stroke yet, all prepared and pending (the love duet that is to be spoken from balcony to garden), Shakespeare pauses to do still better by it; and at the same time fits Mercutio to his true place in the character scheme.[5] To appreciate the device we must first forget the obliging editors with their *Scene i, A lane by the wall of Capulet's orchard. Enter Romeo. . . . He climbs the wall and leaps down within it. . . . Scene ii, Capulet's orchard. Enter Romeo* —for all this has simply obliterated the effect.[6] The *Enter Romeo*

---

[4] But for more argument about the question of act-division that is involved, see p. 323ff.

[5] The Bodleian has recently recovered its original First Folio, and the pages of the balcony-scene are the best thumbed of all.

[6] Rowe is responsible for this. A few of the later editors scented something wrong, but only half-heartedly tried to put it right. Grant White was an honorable exception; but he places Mercutio and Benvolio in the orchard too. Juliet's line

> The orchard walls are high and hard to climb. . . .

discounts that.

alone of the Quartos and Folio is the only authentic stage direction concerning him. What happens when Mercutio and Benvolio arrive in pursuit? He hides somewhere about the stage. He has, they say, "leapt this orchard wall"; but no wall is there, and—more importantly —there is no break in the continuity of the scene, now or later; it should be proof enough that to make one we must cut a rhymed couplet in two. The confusion of whereabouts, such as it is, that is involved, would not trouble the Elizabethans in the least; would certainly not trouble an audience that later on was to see Juliet play half a scene on the upper stage and half on the lower, with no particular change of place implied. The effect, so carefully contrived, lies in Romeo's being well within hearing of all the bawdry now to follow, which has no other dramatic point; and that the chaff is about the chaste Rosaline makes it doubly effective.

Dominating the stage with his lusty presence, vomiting his jolly indecencies, we see the sensual man, Mercutio; while in the background lurks Romeo, a-quiver at them, youth marked for tragedy.[7] His heart's agonizing after Rosaline had been real enough. He has forgotten that! But what awaits him now, with another heart, passionate as his own, to encounter? This is the eloquence of the picture, which is summed up in Romeo's rhyming end to the whole dithyramb as he steals out, looking after the two of them:

> He jests at scars that never felt a wound.

The discord thus struck is perfect preparation for the harmony to come; and Mercutio's ribaldry has hardly died from our ears before Juliet is at her window.

Throughout the famous scene Shakespeare varies and strengthens its harmony and sustains its drama by one small device after another. We must return to more careful study of it. At its finish, the brisk couplet,

> Hence will I to my ghostly father's cell,
> His help to crave, and my dear hap to tell.

brings us to earth again; and the action speeds on, to find a new helmsman in Friar Laurence. His importance to the play is made manifest by the length of his first soliloquy, and Shakespeare is looking forward already, we find, to the potion for Juliet. All goes smoothly and happily; the Friar is sententious, the lovers are ecstatic, Mercutio,

---

[7] The effect will, of course, be intensified if he never leaves our sight, but the mere continuity of the scene, and our sense of him there, produces it.

Benvolio and the Nurse make a merry work-a-day chorus. Only that one note of warning is struck, lightly, casually:

> Tybalt, the kinsman of old Capulet,
> Hath sent a letter to his father's house.

The marriage-scene brings this "movement" to its close.

> *Friar.* So smile the heavens upon this holy act,
> That after-hours with sorrow chide us not!
> *Romeo.* Amen, amen! But come what sorrow can,
> It cannot countervail the exchange of joy
> That one short minute gives me in her sight.
> Do thou but close our hands with holy words,
> Then love-devouring death do what he dare,
> It is enough I may but call her mine.
> *Friar.* These violent delights have violent ends,
> And in their triumph die. . . .

Youth triumphant and defiant, age sadly wise; a scene of quiet consummation, stillness before the storm. We are just halfway through the play.

> Come, come with me, and we will make short work;
> For, by your leaves, you shall not stay alone
> Till holy church incorporate two in one.

But upon this, in immediate, most significant contrast, there stride along Mercutio and Benvolio, swords on hip, armed servants following them, Mercutio with mischief enough a-bubble in him for the prudent Benvolio to be begging:

> I pray thee, good Mercutio, let's retire;
> The day is hot, the Capulets abroad,
> And if we meet we shall not scape a brawl,
> For now, these hot days, is the mad blood stirring.

—and (with one turn of the dramatist's wrist) tragedy is in train.[8]

The scene that follows is the most strikingly effective thing in the play. It comes quickly to its crisis when Romeo enters to encounter Tybalt face to face. For this moment the whole action has been preparing. Consider the constituents of the situation. Tybalt has seen

---

[8] One cannot too strongly insist upon the effect Shakespeare gains by this vivid contrast between scene and scene, swiftly succeeding each other. It is his chief technical resource.

Romeo eying his cousin Juliet from behind a mask and its privilege, and to no good purpose, be sure. But in Benvolio's and Mercutio's eyes he is still the lackadaisical adorer of Rosaline, a scoffer at the famous family quarrel suddenly put to the proof of manhood by a Capulet's insult. We know—we only—that he has even now come from his marriage to Juliet, from the marriage which is to turn these

> households' rancour to pure love.

The moment is made eloquent by a silence. For what is Romeo's answer to be to an insult so complete in its sarcastic courtesy?

> Romeo, the love I bear thee can afford
> No better term than this: Thou art a villain.

Benvolio and Mercutio, Tybalt himself, have no doubt of it; but to us the silence that follows—its lengthening by one pulse-beat mere amazement to them—is all suspense. We know what is in the balance. The moment is, for Romeo, so packed with emotions that the actor may interpret it in half a dozen ways, each legitimate (and by such an endowment we may value a dramatic situation). Does he come from his "one short minute" with Juliet so rapt in happiness that the sting of the insult cannot pierce him, that he finds himself contemplating this Tybalt and his inconsequent folly unmoved? Does he flash into passion and check it, and count the cost to his pride and the scorn of his friends, and count them as nothing, all in an instant? Whatever the effect on him, we, as we watch, can interpret it, no one else guessing. And when he does answer:

> Tybalt, the reason that I have to love thee
> Does much excuse the appertaining rage
> To such a greeting: villain am I none;
> Therefore, farewell; I see thou know'st me not.

the riddle of it is plain only to us. Note that it is the old riddling Romeo that answers, but how changed! We can enjoy, too, the perplexity of those other onlookers and wonder if no one of them will jump to the meaning of the

> good Capulet, which name I tender
> As dearly as my own . . .

But they stand stupent and Romeo passes on.

Upon each character concerned the situation tells differently; yet another test of its dramatic quality. Benvolio stands mute. He is all for peace, but such forbearance who can defend? [9] For Tybalt it is an all but comic letdown. The turning of the cheek makes the smiter look not brave, but ridiculous; and this "courageous captain of compliments" takes ridicule very ill, is the readier, therefore, to recover his fire-eating dignity when Mercutio gives him the chance. And Mercutio, so doing, adds that most important ingredient to the situation, the unforeseen.

> Why the devil came you between us? [he gasps out to Romeo a short minute later] I was hurt under your arm.

But what the devil had he to do with a Capulet-Montague quarrel? The fact is (if one looks back) that he has been itching to read fashion-monger Tybalt a lesson; to show him that *"alla stoccata"* could not carry it away. But *"alla stoccata"* does; and, before we well know where we are, this arbitrary catastrophe gives the sharpest turn yet to the play's action, the liveliest of its figures crumples to impotence before us, the charming rhetoric of the Queen Mab speech has petered out in a savage growl.

The unexpected has its place in drama as well as the plotted and prepared. But observe that Shakespeare uses Mercutio's death to precipitate an essential change in Romeo; and it is this change, not anything extrinsic, that determines the main tragedy. After a parenthesis of scuffle and harsh prose he is left alone on the stage, and a simpler, graver, sterner emotion than any we have known in him yet begins to throb through measured verse.

> This gentleman, the Prince's near ally,
> My very friend, hath got this mortal hurt
> In my behalf; my reputation stained
> With Tybalt's slander—Tybalt, that an hour
> Hath been my cousin. O sweet Juliet,
> Thy beauty hath made me effeminate,
> And in my temper softened valour's steel!

Then he hears that his friend is dead, accepts his destiny—

> This day's black fate on more days doth depend;
> This but begins the woe others must end.

—and so to astonish the blood-intoxicated Tybalt! With a hundred

---

[9] He had been forced to a bout himself with Tybalt the day before; and his description a little later of Romeo,

> With gentle breath, calm look, knees humbly bowed . . .

has exasperation, as well, perhaps, as some politic exaggeration in it.

words, but with expression and action transcending them, Shakespeare has tied the central knot of his play and brought his hero from height to depth.

We are sped on with little relaxation; returning, though, after these close-woven excitements, to declamation with Benvolio's diplomatic apologies (to the play's normal method, that is to say), while a second massed confronting of Montagues and Capulets marks, for reminder, this apex of the action.

We are sped on; and Juliet's ecstasy of expectation, the—

> Gallop apace, you fiery-footed steeds. . . .

—makes the best of contrasts, in matter and manner, to the sternness of Romeo's banishing. A yet sharper contrast follows quickly with the Nurse's coming, carrying the ladder of cords (the highway to the marriage bed, for emphasis of irony), standing mute a minute while Juliet stares, then breaking incontinently into her

> he's dead, he's dead, he's dead.

From now—with hardly a lapse to quiet—one scene will compete with the next in distraction till Friar Laurence comes to still the outcry of mourning over the drugged Juliet on her bed. The lovers compete in despair and desperate hope; Capulet precipitates confusion; the Friar himself turns foolhardy. All the action is shot through with haste and violence, and with one streak at least of gratuitous savagery besides. For if the plot demands Capulet's capricious tyrannies it does not need Lady Capulet's impulse to send a man after Romeo to poison him. But the freshly kindled virus of hatred (does Shakespeare feel?) must now spend itself even to exhaustion. From this point to the play's end, indeed, the one reposeful moment is when Romeo's

> dreams presage some joyful news at hand . . .

But the next is only the more shattering; and from then to the last tragic accidents it is a tale of yet worse violence, yet more reckless haste.[10]

[10] The slaughtering of Paris is wanton and serves little dramatic purpose. Lady Montague is dead also by the end of the play (though no one gives much heed to that) and Q1 even informs us that

> young Benvolio is deceased too.

Here, however, the slaughter is probably less arbitrary—from one point of view. The actors had other parts to play. By the time Q2 has come into being Shakespeare knows better than to call attention to Benvolio's absence. Who notices it? But his audiences—a proportion of them—no doubt loved a holocaust for its own sake, and he was not above indulging them now and then.

It is, of course, in the end a tragedy of mischance. Shakespeare was bound by his story, was doubtless content to be; and how make it otherwise? Nevertheless, we discern his deeper dramatic sense, which was to shape the maturer tragedies, already in revolt. Accidents make good incidents, but tragedy determined by them has no significance. So he sets out, we see, in the shaping of his characters, to give all likelihood to the outcome. It is by pure ill-luck that Friar John's speed to Mantua is stayed while Balthasar reaches Romeo with the news of Juliet's death; but it is Romeo's headlong recklessness that leaves Friar Laurence no time to retrieve the mistake. It is, by a more subtle turn, Juliet's overacted repentance of her "disobedient opposition," which prompts the delighted Capulet to

> have this knot knit up to-morrow morning.

And this difference of a day proves also to be the difference between life and death.

Before ever the play begins, the chorus foretells its ending. The star-crossed lovers must, we are warned,

> with their death bury their parents' strife.

But Shakespeare is not content with the plain theme of an innocent happiness foredoomed. He makes good dramatic use of it. Our memory of the Prologue, echoing through the first scenes of happy encounter, lends them a poignancy which makes their beauties doubly beautiful. The sacrament of the marriage, with Romeo's invocation—

> Do thou but close our hands with holy words,
> Then love-devouring death do what he dare,
> It is enough I may but call her mine.

—read into it, stands as symbol of the sacrifice that all love and happiness must make to death. But character also is fate; it is, at any rate, the more dramatic part of it, and the life of Shakespeare's art is to lie in the manifesting of this. These two lovers, then, must in themselves be prone to disaster. They are never so freed from the accidents of their story as his later touch would probably have made them. But by the time he has brought them to their full dramatic stature we cannot—accidents or no—imagine a happy ending, or a Romeo and Juliet married and settled as anything but a burlesque.

So, the turning point of Mercutio's death and Tybalt's and Romeo's banishing being past, Shakespeare brings all his powers to bear upon the molding of the two figures to inevitable tragedy; and the producer of the play must note with care how the thing is done. To begin with, over a succession of scenes—in all but one of which either Romeo or Juliet is concerned—there is no relaxing of tension, vehemence or speed; for every flagging moment in them there is some fresh spur, they reinforce each other too, the common practice of contrast between scene and scene is more or less foregone.[11] And the play's declamatory method is heightened, now into rhapsody, now into a veritable dervish-whirling of words.

Shakespeare's practical ability—while he still hesitates to discard it —to turn verbal conventions to lively account is shown to the full in the scene between Juliet and the Nurse, with which this stretch of the action begins—his success, also his failure. The passage in which Juliet's bewildered dread finds expression in a cascade of puns is almost invariably cut on the modern stage, and one may sympathize with the actress who shirks it. But it is, in fact, word-play perfectly adapted to dramatic use; and to the Elizabethans puns were not neces-sarily comic things.

> Hath Romeo slain himself? Say thou but "I,"
> And that bare vowel "I" shall poison more
> Than the death-dealing eye of cockatrice:
> I am not I, if there be such an "I,"
> Or those eyes shut that make thee answer "I."
> If he be slain, say "I"; or if not, no:
> Brief sounds determine of my weal or woe.

Shut our minds to its present absurdity (but it is no more absurd than any other bygone fashion), allow for the rhetorical method, and con-sider the emotional effect of the word-music alone—what a vivid ex-pression of the girl's agonized mind it makes, this intoxicated con-fusion of words and meanings! The whole scene is written in terms of conventional rhetoric. We pass from play upon words to play upon phrase, paradox, antithesis.

> O serpent heart, hid with a flowering face!
> Did ever dragon keep so fair a cave?
> Beautiful tyrant; fiend angelical!
> Dove-feathered raven! wolfish ravening lamb!
> Despised substance of divinest show!
> Just opposite to what thou justly seem'st;
> A damned saint, an honourable villain! . . .

[11] I say deliberately "in all but one," not two, for the reason I give later.

The boy-Juliet was here evidently expected to give a display of virtuosity comparable to the singing of a *scena* in a mid-nineteenth century opera. That there was no danger of the audience finding it ridiculous we may judge by Shakespeare's letting the Nurse burlesque the outcry with her

> There's no trust,
> No faith, no honesty in men; all perjured,
> All forsworn, all naught, all dissemblers!

For it is always a daring thing to sandwich farce with tragedy; and though Shakespeare was fond of doing it, obviously he would not if the tragedy itself were trembling on the edge of farce.

The weakness of the expedient shows later, when, after bringing us from rhetoric to pure drama with the Nurse's

> Will you speak well of him that killed your cousin?

and Juliet's flashing answer,

> Shall I speak ill of him that is my husband?

—one of those master touches that clarify and consummate a whole situation—Shakespeare must needs take us back to another screed of the sort which now shows meretricious by comparison. For a finish, though, we have the fine simplicity, set in formality, of

> *Juliet.* Where is my father and my mother, Nurse?
> *Nurse.* Weeping and wailing over Tybalt's corse:
>   Will you go to them? I will bring you thither.
> *Juliet.* Wash they his wounds with tears! Mine shall be spent,
>   When theirs are dry, for Romeo's banishment.
>   Take up those cords. Poor ropes, you are beguiled,
>   Both you and I, for Romeo is exiled.
>   He made you for a highway to my bed,
>   But I, a maid, die maiden-widowed.

By one means and another, he has now given us a new and a passionate and desperate Juliet, more fitted to her tragic end.

In the scene that follows, we have desperate Romeo in place of desperate Juliet, with the Friar to lift it to dignity at the finish and to push the story a short step forward. The maturer Shakespeare would not, perhaps, have coupled such similar scenes so closely; but both likeness and repetition serve his present purpose.

To appraise the value of the next effect he makes we must again visualize the Elizabethan stage.[12] Below

Enter Capulet, Lady Capulet and Paris.

With Tybalt hardly buried, Juliet weeping for him, it has been no time for urging Paris' suit.

> 'Tis very late [says Capulet], she'll not come down to-night:
> I promise you, but for your company,
> I should have been a-bed an hour ago.

Paris takes his leave, asks Lady Capulet to commend him to her daughter. She answers him:

> I will, and know her mind early to-morrow;
> To-night she's mewed up to her heaviness.

But *we* know that, at this very moment, Romeo and Juliet, bride and bridegroom, are in each other's arms.

Paris is actually at the door, when, with a sudden impulse, Capulet recalls him.[13]

> Sir Paris, I will make a desperate tender
> Of my child's love. I think she will be ruled
> In all respects by me; nay, more, I doubt it not.
> Wife, go you to her ere you go to bed;
> Acquaint her here of my son Paris' love,
> And bid her, mark you me, on Wednesday next . . .

And by that sudden impulse, so lightly obeyed, the tragedy is precipitated. Capulet, bitten by an idea, is in a ferment.

> Well, Wednesday is too soon;
> O' Thursday let it be:—o' Thursday, tell her,
> She shall be married to this noble earl.
> Will you be ready? Do you like this haste? . . .

(In a trice he has shaken off the mourning uncle and turned jovial, roguish father-in-law.)

---

[12] But we must do this throughout.

[13] And we may rely on this as one of the very few authenticated pieces of Shakespearean "business." For Q1 says,

> *Paris offers to goe in and Capolet calls him againe.*

If the presumed reporter watching the performance thought it important and had the time to note this down, it must have been markedly done.

> Well, get you gone! O' Thursday be it then.—
> Go you to Juliet ere you go to bed,
> Prepare her, wife, against this wedding day. . . .

(What, we are asking, will Lady Capulet find if she does go?)

> Farewell, my lord.—Light to my chamber, ho!
> Afore me, it's so very late
> That we may call it early by and by:—
> Good-night.

Now comes the well-prepared effect. Hardly have the three vanished below, bustling and happy; when with

> Wilt thou begone? It is not yet near day. . . .

Juliet and Romeo appear at the window above, clinging together, agonized in the very joy of their union, but all ignorant of this new and deadly blow which (again) *we* know is to fall on them.

Only the unlocalized stage is capable of just such an effect as this. Delay in the shifting of scenery may be overcome by the simple lifting of a front scene to discover Romeo and Juliet in her chamber behind it; but Shakespeare's audience had not even to shift their imaginations from one place to another. The lower stage was anywhere downstairs in Capulet's house. The upper stage was associated with Juliet; it had served for her balcony and had been put to no other use.[14] So while Capulet is planning the marriage with Paris not only will our thoughts have been traveling to her, but our eyes may have rested speculatively, too, on those closed curtains above.

Shakespeare speeds his action all he can. Capulet, itching with his new idea, gives invaluable help. Romeo has hardly dropped from the balcony before Lady Capulet is in her daughter's room.[15] Capulet himself comes on her heels. It is barely daybreak and he has not been to bed. (The night is given just that confused chronology such feverish nights seem to have.) With morning Juliet flies to the Friar, to find Paris already with him, the news already agitating him; she herself is the more agitated by the unlooked-for meeting with Paris. The encounter between them, with its equivoque, oddly echoes her first encounter with Romeo; but it is another Juliet that now plays a suitor

---

[14] The musicians at Capulet's supper would probably have sat in it; but this is hardly a dramatic use. Nor does the mere association with Juliet *localize* it. There is no such scientific precision in the matter.

[15] For the stage business involved here, see p. 327ff.

with words. It is a more deeply passionate Juliet, too, that turns from
Paris' formal kiss with

> Oh, shut the door, and when thou hast done so,
> Come weep with me; past hope, past cure, past help!

than so passionately greeted the news of Tybalt's death and Romeo's
banishment. Child she may still be, but she is now a wife.

We should count the Friar's long speech with which he gives her
the potion, in which he tells her his plan, as a sort of strong pillar of
rhetoric, from which the play's action is to be swung to the next strong
pillar, the speech (in some ways its counterpart) in which Juliet nerves
herself to the drinking it. For, with Romeo removed for the moment,
the alternating scene falls to Capulet and his bustlings; these are admirable as contrast, but of no dramatic power, and the action at this
juncture must be well braced and sustained.

We come now to another and still more important effect, that is
(yet again) only to be realized in the theater for which it was designed.
The curtains of the inner stage are drawn back to show us Juliet's bed.
Her nurse and her mother leave her; she drinks the potion, and—says
that note-taker at the performance, whose business it was, presumably,
to let his employers know exactly how all the doubtful bits were done—

> *She falls upon the bed within the curtains.*

There has been argument upon argument whether this means the
curtains of the bed or of the inner stage—which would then close on
her. The difference in dramatic effect will be of degree and not kind.
What Shakespeare aims at in the episodes that follow is to keep us
conscious of the bed and its burden; while in front of it, Capulet and
the servants, Lady Capulet and the Nurse pass hither and thither,
laughing and joking over the preparation for the wedding, till the
bridal music is playing, till, to the very sound of this, the Nurse bustles
up to draw back the curtains and disclose the girl there stark and
still.[16]

This is one of the chief dramatic effects of the play; and it can only
be gained by preserving the continuity of the action, with its agonies

---

[16] To Shakespeare's audience it would make little matter which sort of curtains
they were. A closed bed standing shadowed on the inner stage is at once to be
ignored and recognized. We also, with a little practice, can ignore it, with Capulet;
though to our more privileged gaze there it significantly is, in suspended animation,
as it were, till the Nurse, fingering its curtains, brings it back to dramatic life, as
we have known she must, as we have been waiting breathlessly for her to do.
Whether they should be bed curtains or stage curtains is a matter of convention,
a question of more imagination or less.

and absurdities cheek by jowl, with that bridal music sharpening the irony at the last. It is a comprehensive effect, extending from the drinking of the potion to the Nurse's parrot scream when she finds Juliet stiff and cold; and even beyond, to the coming of the bridegroom and his train, through the long-spoken threnody, to the farce of the ending —which helps to remind us that, after all, Juliet is not dead. It is one scene, one integral stretch of action; and its common mutilation by *Scene iv. Hall in Capulet's house . . . Scene v. Juliet's chamber. Enter Nurse . . .*, with the consequences involved, is sheer editorial murder.

Modern producers, as a rule, do even worse by it than the editors. They bring down a curtain upon a display of virtuosity in a "potion-scene," long drawn out, worried to bits, and leave us to recover till they are ready with Romeo in Mantua and the apothecary. And even faithful Shakespeareans have little good to say of that competition in mourning between Paris and Capulet, Lady Capulet and the Nurse. It has been branded as deliberate burlesque. It is assuredly no more so than was Juliet's outbreak against Romeo upon Tybalt's death; to each, we notice, the Nurse provides a comic, characteristic echo, which would have little point if it did not contrast, rather absurdly, with the rest. Burlesque, of a sort, comes later with Peter and the musicians; Shakespeare would not anticipate this effect, and so equivocally! The passage does jar a little; but we must remember that he is working here in a convention that has gone somewhat stale with him, and constrainedly; and that he can call now on no such youthful, extravagant passion as Juliet's or Romeo's to make the set phrases live. The situation is dramatically awkward, besides; in itself it mocks at the mourners, and Friar Laurence's reproof of them, which comes unhappily near to cant, hardly clarifies it. Shakespeare comes lamely out; but he went sincerely in. Nor does the farce of Peter and the musicians, conventional as it is, stray wholly beyond likelihood. Peter is comic in his grief; but many people are. Will Kempe, it may be, had to have his fling; but this part of the scene has its dramatic value, too. It develops and broadens—vulgarizes, if you will—the irony of the bridal music brought to the deathbed; and, the traditional riddle-me-ree business done with (and Will Kempe having "brought off an exit" amid cheers), there is true sting in the tail of it:

> *First Musician.* What a pestilent knave is this same!
> *Second Musician.* Hang him, Jack! Come, we'll in here; tarry for the mourners, and stay dinner.

And, of course, it eases the strain before tragedy gets its final grip of us. We find Romeo in Mantua poised upon happiness before his last

sudden plunge to despair and death. Shakespeare has now achieved
simplicity in his treatment of him, brought the character to maturity
and his own present method to something like perfection. What can
be simpler, more obvious yet more effective than the dream with its
flattering presage of good news—

> I dreamt my lady came and found me dead—
> Strange dream, that gives a dead man leave to think!—
> And breathed such life with kisses in my lips,
> That I revived, and was an emperor. . . .

—followed incontinently by Balthasar's

> Her body sleeps in Capels' monument,
> And her immortal part with angels lives. . . .

So much for dreams! So much for life and its flatteries! And the buying
of the poison shows us a Romeo grown out of all knowledge away
from the sentimental, phrase-making adorer of Rosaline.

> There is thy gold; worse poison to men's souls,
> Doing more murder in this loathsome world
> Than these poor compounds that thou mayst not sell:
> I sell thee poison, thou hast sold me none.

This aging of Romeo is marked by more than one touch. To the contemptuous Tybalt he was a boy; now Paris to him, when they meet, is
to be "good gentle youth."

Then, after one more needed link in the story has been riveted,
we reach the play's last scene. Producers are accustomed to eliminate
most of this, keeping the slaughtering of Paris as a prelude, concen-
trating upon Romeo's death and Juliet's, possibly providing a sort of
symbolic picture of Montagues and Capulets reconciled at the end.
This is all very well, and saves us the sweet kernel of the nut, no doubt;
but it happens not to be the scene that Shakespeare devised. To appreciate that we must once more visualize the stage for which it was
devised. The authorities are in dispute upon several points here, but
only of detail. Juliet lies entombed in the inner stage; that is clear.
The outer stage stands for the churchyard; as elastically as it stood
before for the street or the courtyard of Capulet's house in which the
Maskers marched about, while the serving-men coming forth with their
napkins converted it, as vaguely, into the hall. Now it is as near to the
tomb or as far from it as need be, and the action on it (it is the larger
part of this that is usually cut) will be prominent and important. The
tomb itself is the inner stage, closed in, presumably, by gates which

Romeo breaks open, through the bars of which Paris casts his flowers. Juliet herself lies like a recumbent effigy upon a rectangular block of stone, which must be low enough and wide enough for Romeo to lie more or less beside her; and other such monuments, uneffigied, Tybalt's among them, may surround her.[17]

Once more Shakespeare hurries us through a whole night of confusion; from the coming of Paris, the cheated bridegroom, and Romeo, the robbed husband, to this ghastly bride-bed, through one tragic miscarrying after another, to the Prince's summing-up:

> A glooming peace this morning with it brings. . . .

All is confusion; only the regularity of the verse keeps it from running away. Paris is fearful of disturbance,[18] and Romeo, when he comes, is strained beyond endurance or control. It is not till he has fleshed the edge of his desperation upon poor Paris, till he is sobered by seeing what he has done, that, armed securely with his poison, he can take his calm farewell. Once he is dead, confusion is let loose. The Friar approaches with

> Saint Francis be my speed! How oft to-night
> Have my old feet stumbled at graves! . . .

Balthasar and he whisper and tremble. Then Juliet wakes; but before he can speak to her, the watch are heard coming. He flies; and she has but time to find the empty phial in Romeo's hand, bare time to find his dagger and stab herself before they appear, and the hunt is up:

> *Paris' Page.* This is the place; there, where the torch doth burn.
> *Captain of the Watch.* The ground is bloody; search about the churchyard:
>   Go, some of you, whoe'er you find, attach.

---

[17] We need not comb the text for objections to this arrangement, which is practicable, while no other is. For an explanation of

> Why I *descend* into this bed of death . . .

for instance, we have only to turn to Brooke's poem (lines 2620–2630). The frontispiece to Rowe's edition of the play is (incidentally) worth observing. It does not show a stage-setting, even a Restoration stage-setting, but the tomb itself may well be the sort of thing that was used. Paris and Romeo, it can be seen, wear semi-Roman costume. Is this, by any hazardous chance, explicable by the fact that Otway's perversion of the play, *Caius Marius*, was then current in the theaters (*Romeo and Juliet* itself was not, it seems, revived till 1744; and then much altered)? Did Du Guernier begin his drawing with the Roman lovers in his mind?

[18] For no compelling reason; but Shakespeare felt the need of striking this note at once, since a first note will tend to be the dominant one.

Pitiful sight! here lies the county slain,
And Juliet bleeding, warm and newly dead,
Who here hath lain this two days buried.[19]
Go, tell the Prince; run to the Capulets;
Raise up the Montagues; some others search. . . .

Cries, confusion, bustle; some of the watch bring back Balthasar, some others the Friar; the Prince arrives with his train, the Capulets surge in, the Montagues; the whole front stage is filled with the coming and going, while, in dreadful contrast, plain to our sight within the tomb, the torchlight flickering on them, Romeo and Juliet lie still.[20]

The play is not over, another hundred lines go to its finishing; and, to appease our modern impatience of talk when no more is to be done, here, if nowhere else, the producer will wield the blue pencil doughtily. Why should the Friar recount at length—after saying he'll be brief, moreover!—what we already know, with Balthasar to follow suit, and Paris' page to follow him? There are half a dozen good reasons. Shakespeare neither could nor would, of course, bring a play to a merely catastrophic end; the traditions of his stage no less than its conditions forbade this. Therefore the Prince's authoritative

Seal up the mouth of outrage for a while,
Till we can clear these ambiguities,
And know their spring, their head, their true descent;
And then I will be general of your woes,
And lead you even to death: meantime forbear. . . .

with which he stills a tumult that threatens otherwise to end the play, as it began, in bloody rough-and-tumble—this is the obvious first note of a formal full-close. But the Friar's story must be told, because the play's true end is less in the death of the star-crossed lovers than in the burying of their parents' strife; and as it has been primarily a play of tangled mischances, the unraveling of these, the bringing home of their meaning to the sufferers by them, is a natural part of its process. How else lead up to the Prince's

Where be these enemies? Capulet—Montague!
See what a scourge is laid upon your hate. . . .

[19] Another instance of Shakespeare's use of time for momentary effect—or of his carelessness. Or will someone find a subtle stroke of character in the Watchman's inaccuracy?

[20] It is of some interest to note that *Antony and Cleopatra* ends with a similar stage effect.

and to the solution with Capulet's

O brother Montague, give me thy hand. . . .

For us also—despite our privileged vision—it has been a play of confused, passion-distorted happenings, and the Friar's plain tale makes
the simple pity of them clear, and sends us away with this foremost
in our minds. Again, declamation is the norm of the play's method,
and it is natural to return to that for a finish. Finally, as it is a tragedy
less of character than of circumstance, upon circumstance its last emphasis naturally falls. Yet, all this admitted, one must own that the
penultimate stretch of the writing, at least, is poor in quality. Shakespeare has done well by his story and peopled it with passionate life.
But, his impulse flagging, his artistry is still found immature.

Shakespeare's Young Lovers

by Elmer Edgar Stoll

. . . Shakespeare's comedy and tragedy alike are not studies, not human documents; and the passion [of love], arising at first sight, is a simple reaction, to the woman's beauty or the man's noble mien. It is an affair of the imagination, not of the intellect, and, apparently, neither the result of a community of tastes or aspirations, on the one hand, nor the cause of a new envisagement of life or adjustment to it, on the other. In this respect, consequently, the plays are scarcely dramas. The passion is not pitted against others such as ambition or revenge; not brought into conflict with ideals such as honour, or with duties such as those to parents or society. It is generally both spontaneous and contagious, untroubled by fear or doubt or questioning. In short, it is . . . in a state of health and equilibrium, and that does not lend itself to drama; it is in a state of health and happiness to the point of charm and beauty, and that does lend itself to poetry.

Now all this is true of Romeo and Juliet, though being, unlike the other lovers with whom we are to deal, in a tragedy, they are in the external action more deeply involved. They fall in love at sight and for ever, and, in their own personal relations, are material only for poetry, not for psychology but for character-drawing. Their struggle is not with each other, nor within themselves, but only with their quarrelling families, against the stars. They do not misunderstand or deceive, allure or elude, suspect or tantalize, turn, naturally or unnaturally, from love to hatred or wreak themselves upon each other, as both in drama and in life lovers not uncommonly do; nor are they swayed or inwardly troubled by their inheritance of enmity, or by filial fealty, or for more than a moment by thoughts of a Capulet's blood on Romeo's hand. There is not even the veil of a disguise between them; and the family prejudices or obligations which for

From "Romeo and Juliet," in Shakespeare's Young Lovers by Elmer Edgar Stoll (New York: Oxford University Press, 1937), pp. 3-5, 21-32. Reprinted by permission of the publisher.

Corneille or Racine would, as in the *Cid,* have been the making of the drama, the dramatist recognizes but avoids. Or is it the lovers themselves that fatefully avoid them, ignore them? "All for Love and The World Well Lost" might be the title, though in a different sense from Dryden's; and it is not their self-centred absorption and infatuation or any other internal entanglement that brings them to their death, but (the poet makes clear) the feud and destiny.

There is no tragic fault, or (as we shall see) none in the ordinary sense of the word. Certainly there is none of a social or psychological sort. The play itself, like most of Shakespeare's love stories, is conceived in terms not only of poetry but of romance, of *amor vincit omnia;* and these young and tender things are no more to be judged for disobeying and deceiving their parents than Desdemona or Imogen, Florizel or Perdita, Ferdinand or Miranda, who also do. They come to ruin not because, as Butcher says, "in their newfound rapture they act in defiance of all external obligations." They so act, to be sure, but the observation has point only as registering a distinction between romance and realism; in so far as their recklessness occurs to us it is meant to redound to the lovers' credit. The point of the play—the wonder of the story—is, not how such a love can arise out of hatred and then triumph over it in death, but that it does.

* * *

The great emotional situation is what Shakespeare was seeking; and in this early and lesser tragedy Romeo is swept off his feet by love as, in the later ones, Othello, Posthumus, and Leontes are by jealousy, Macbeth by ambition, Hamlet by the Ghost's revelations and command, and Lear by thwarted paternal affection. And for the full impression we need—we must have—no analysis or previously indicated inclination, but a Romeo thinking, the moment before, of another woman when we hear him break out at the ball, at the sight of Juliet:

> O, she doth teach the torches to burn bright!

and we need a Juliet who has already averred that matrimony is an honour that she dreams not of, when she bids her Nurse

> Go ask his name.—If he be marrièd,
> My grave is like to be my wedding-bed . . .

a Juliet and a Romeo each aware, the moment after, that the other is an enemy. For the full impression, moreover, we need the traditional, the simple and sensuous motive of the maiden's beauty. With the full force of the impression a more spiritual motive, even could it here be adequately provided, would interfere.

And the emotional situation is justified or made acceptable, as often in Shakespeare, not by analysis and realism, but by stage management, by poetry, by the fitness of the situation in the world that the poet has created. Instead of a definite psychological transition from Rosaline to Juliet, there is, for plausibility's sake, a slight interval after Romeo's outcry (which the hero may be supposed to use for reflection and read-justment) bridged by the quarrel between the testy Tybalt and the hospitable Capulet; and instead of the long and tedious process of getting acquainted and making love, there is a wooing which is lifted above the level of life by rime and brought within the compass of a sonnet. This way of courting and mating is appropriate in Shake-speare's romantic Verona, as Othello's sudden jealousy is in a Venice and a Cyprus where Iago enjoys such a reputation, or Imogen's credit-ing Iachimo after Posthumus has, by his letter of introduction, done the same. That the youth and the maiden should fall in love at sight is not out of keeping with their at once making the fact known to each other, with her doing more than the girl's ordinary share of the wooing and his forgetting Rosaline on the spot; with the thought of both that this is a matter of union or of death, in disregard of all prudential or practical considerations, in defiance of the stars; and with their high poetical ways of talking generally as well as the roman-tic incidents and setting—masques, balls, tempestuous quarrels and duels, endearments in the moonlight and bidding adieu at dawn, a wedding in a Friar's cell and a ladder to reach the wedding-bed, and thereupon the sleeping-potion, the burial alive to escape the accepted suitor, the reunion only in the grave. It is a thoroughly romantic world (though a more turbulent and passionate one), as in the *Mid-summer Night's Dream, The Merchant of Venice, As You Like It, Twelfth Night,* and nearly all the rest, where more or less similarly the premature falling in love is made plausible.

Furthermore, the motive for it, the maiden's beauty, is made ade-quate and convincing by its retention—the maiden's attraction is the wife's—and its retention is owing to its poetic and dramatic advan-tages. In the tomb scene it is still Juliet's "beauty" that moves the hero, making the vault a lantern, "a feasting presence full of light." Upon that death "hath had no power," its "ensign yet is crimson in thy lips and in thy cheeks, and death's pale flag is not advanced there." "Thou art not conquer'd," in his immortal words. A more soberly edifying and satisfying spectacle might have been made out of his considering Juliet's spiritual qualities; her soul it might have been that is not conquered; but Romeo is like Othello, yet to come. In that tragedy the motivation, at the outset, is less traditional, though as summarily romantic:

> She lov'd me for the dangers I had pass'd,
> And I lov'd her that she did pity them.

But presently for him too the woman's charm is her beauty; and it is by this sensuous simplification that his love for her is kept before us in the midst of his jealous anguish:—"the fair devil"; "lest her body and beauty unprovide my mind again"; "lest being like one of heaven the devils themselves should fear to seize thee"; "Oh, thou weed, who art so lovely fair and smell'st so sweet, that the sense aches at thee." Better this than any exposition.

The method, then, is imaginative and immediate, impulsive and emotional, dramatic or at least structural and poetic, not (happily) psychological or sociological. The motives, in so far as there are any—Juliet's beauty and her particular features—are dwelt upon but to start the story and support the situation; and that the lovers are fitted for each other appears indirectly and incidentally—they themselves are not concerned about it—as with Benedick and Beatrice, Orlando and Rosalind, Florizel and Perdita, Ferdinand and Miranda. If not otherwise, by their fruits we know them,—health out of lovesickness, daring and resourcefulness out of inexperience. But the chief thing is that we should be made to feel the greatness of their love and then in each of them find warrant for it. If Othello is called noble, Desdemona gentle, and Iago (in his villainous hypocrisy) "honest," we must, in order to yield the author full credence, be convinced of it in our own right. So we must be impressed directly by Romeo's and Juliet's reality and charm; for ourselves we must be led to acknowledge that each is worth the winning; and in this play, as in the other and in Shakespeare generally, that is done, again, not by analysis, but by poetry and the quality and individuality of their speech.

To be sure, they are characterized by their deeds as well (where these are not determined by the requirements of the plot) and by their sentiments. Both lovers are poetical and imaginative; but Romeo is more a prey to his imagination and is less compact and practical, less ready and resolute, as young men commonly are. It is Juliet that first thinks of matrimony and the means to secure it, whether in the ballroom or on the balcony. It is she that arranges for wedding, priest, and means of communication, while Romeo is still rapt and lost in love's young dream. (No wonder, after passing from out of one dream

into another!) When marriage to Paris is threatened she welcomes any
escape, by knife or poison or a slumber in a tomb; when, at the end,
she wakens from it, her words are few, her deed unhesitating. And like
a girl or woman, she lives more in her affections and prejudices, is
more personal and concrete. She is far more troubled at finding Romeo
to be a Montague than he is at finding her to be a Capulet; her grief
at the killing of Tybalt, though genuine, is at once overwhelmed by
resentment against the Nurse for abusing her lover. Only a new feeling
can subdue the old. Twice she curses the Nurse, both now and when
she is advised to give up Romeo for Paris. "Ancient damnation" is
equivalent to "damned old woman," though not so vulgar; and that
is not the only time that her language is passionately but appropriately
improper. Yet, true to her sex, she is both more explosive than Romeo
and, when need be, more self-contained. On the second occasion she
keeps her anger to herself until the Nurse has left the room, just as
she presently does her true feelings and purposes from her father and
mother. And it is the same concreteness in her frank and ardent expectation of her wedding-night. Sanctioned by the highly moral Coleridge and Hazlitt, this surely need not be defended today; even at this
seat and refuge of classical learning people read, I dare say with some
measure of approval, not many, I hope, but the best of contemporary
novels, and those who don't, why, they may go back to their Catullus,
Tibullus, and Propertius, to Theocritus and the Anthology. Here,
needless to say, is nothing like the frankness there; and if purity is a
matter of balance, of equipoise and sanity, of the ideal to match and
animate the real, then certainly in Juliet we have it, who thinks of
Romeo not only as a man but as a kindred spirit, and who, before
she knows of him, answering her mother on the subject of matrimony,
speaks from out of the rare upper region of romance:

> It is an honour that I dream not of.

She is not in love with love, as Romeo has been; nearly three centuries later, Charlotte Brontë, in *Jane Eyre,* gave offence to her readers
by presenting her heroine in that state, permissible enough for the
hero; and if Shakespeare had attempted the like, how he would have
put her at the mercy of the philosophical Teutons! This virginal innocence of hers is thrown into high relief by the Nurse's chipping in—

> An honour! were not I thine only nurse,
> I would say thou hadst sucked wisdom from thy teat;

much as her conjugal devotion is two days later—time and life move
swiftly here—by the Nurse's counsel to give up Romeo and marry

again. All in all she is evidently a jewel worth the winning; and in poetry, at any rate, would not be more so if, instead of surrendering to love at discretion, she had deliberately and circumspectly considered whether the youth possessed the solid and substantial qualities desirable in a husband and father.

It is mainly, however, in their speech or methods of expression that the finer discrimination of their characters and the elements of their charm reside. Romeo's imagination flies higher, ranges more widely, and it is he that has the figure of adventure:

> I am no pilot; yet wert thou as far
> As that vast shore wash'd with the farthest sea,
> I should adventure for such merchandise . . .

which he echoes in the tomb scene:

> Thou desperate pilot, now at once run on
> The dashing rocks thy sea-sick weary bark

just as it is he that has visions of glory like this in the tomb:

> Thou art not conquer'd, beauty's ensign yet
> Is crimson in thy lips and in thy cheeks,
> And death's pale flag is not advancèd there,

and this on facing the dawn after the wedding-night:

> Night's candles are burnt out and jocund day
> Stands tiptoe on the misty mountain tops.

In both the later passages there is a fuller and richer melody than in the earlier ones. It is proper that such an experience as his should have left its impress upon him.

Juliet's imagination is simpler, less frankly poetical but more naïve and individual; and it is pervaded with her girlish playfulness, which, except in anger, seldom deserts her. As in her wooing, for of that she does her share:

> 'Tis almost morning, I would have thee gone;—
> And yet no farther than a wanton's bird;
> That lets it hop a little from her hand,
> Like a poor prisoner in his twisted gyves,
> And with a silken thréad plúcks it báck agáin . . .

(There she plucks it!) And even in meditating up amid the constellations:

> Come, gentle night, come, loving, black-brow'd night,
> Give me my Romeo; and when he shall die,
> Take him and cut him out in little stars,
> And he will make the face of heaven so fine
> That all the world will be in love with night,
> And pay no worship to the garish sun . . .

Both make love wittily and humorously, as most of Shakespeare's young people do; but Juliet's playful or caressing, confiding or cajoling manner is something that is more native and inseparable, as when she coaxes the Nurse to tell her the news,

> Sweet, sweet, sweet nurse, tell me, what says my love?

or when she takes refuge with her for comfort:

> Cómfort me, cóunsel me
>
>   *   *   *   *   *   *   *   *   *
>
> What sáy'st thou? Hast thou not a wórd of jóy?
> Sòme cómfort, núrse?

With Angelica she is a child, and still more than most charming women she is something of a child with her lover. "I would I were thy bird," whispers Romeo:

> Sweet, so would I;
> Yet I should kill thee with much cherishing.

The great effect, however, the perfect, unexpected touch, upon which I have twice elsewhere commented but am all the more eager to do so again, is as she wakes to find the cup in his hand. "O churl," she murmurs,—"bad boy"—

> O churl! drunk all, and left no friendly drop
> To help me after!

To him she speaks, not of him. He is only a step away, in a moment she herself will take it, and on his heedlessness she rallies him. Whether this is imagination in her or a childish want of it, there is no doubt what it is in the poet himself as he now sees her lips lifting at the corners as of old.

Though kept identical, however, the pair, as I have already intimated, develop, too rapidly for realism but not for poetry. "Go, counsellor," she mutters after the Nurse has advised compliance:

> Thou and my bosom henceforth shall be twain.

Give me, she bids the Friar when he proposes the dangerous potion,

> Give me, give me! O, tell not me of fear!

she, who a few moments before had been begging for comfort. But the greater change is in Romeo, from lovesickness back to his lively witty self that we have not yet known, but Mercutio has and delights in, then to the self-restraint under Tybalt's insults, then to the manly retaliation for Mercutio's death, then to the calm of a desperate resolve as he receives the news:

> Is it even so? Then I defy you, stars.

> Well, Juliet, I will lie with thee to-night.

He is a man now, not a lad; there is now no wailing or ranting as in the Friar's cell. And in the changes of mood and tone that follow there is no more of the extravagance or egotism of passion. He can think of others—considers the misery of the apothecary and wonders at him:

> Art thou so base and full of wretchedness
> And fear'st to die?

and, paying him, bids him "buy food and get thyself in flesh." As before the tomb he tells Balthasar to be gone, he adds,

> Live, and be prosperous; and farewell, good fellow;

and Paris, who interposes, he beseeches,

> Good gentle youth, tempt not a desperate man.

Though Paris is as yet unknown to him, when he falls, begging to be laid with Juliet, Romeo answers at once, "In faith, I will," and then recognizing him, in an outburst of generosity:

> What said my man, when my betossed soul
> Did not attend him as we rode? I think
> He told me Paris should have married Juliet.
> Said he not so? Or did I dream it so?
> Or am I mad, hearing him talk of Juliet,
> To think it was so? O, give me thy hand,
> One writ with me in sour misfortune's book!
> I'll bury thee in a triumphant grave . . .

So in the tomb, at the sight of Tybalt in his bloody sheet, he cries,

> Forgive me, cousin!

He is even so grown up and self-forgetful in his passion as to let his wits have play, or, as he expresses it, be a little "merry." When at the purchase of the poison, the Apothecary excuses himself—

> My poverty, not my will, consents,

he catches him up and helps him through the loophole—

> I pay thy poverty, and not thy will;

and now, even as he drinks, he remembers him and his assurances—

> O true apothecary!
> Thy drugs are quick.

A man, he has at the supreme moment, more thoughts than a single one, like Raleigh, Sir Thomas More, the Emperor Vespasian, and like Hamlet, who, under the shadow of death, bandies words with the Gravedigger and Osric. He is not a Werther, though at the outset he bade fair to be.

Shakespeare's Experimental Tragedy

by H. B. Charlton

In their general structure and idea, the three tragedies so far reviewed [*Titus Andronicus, Richard III, Richard II*] were in the current dramatic tradition of their day. But *Romeo and Juliet* is a departure, a comprehensive experiment. It links the English stage to the Renaissance tragedy which by precept and by practice Cinthio[1] in the middle of the sixteenth century had established in Italy.

Cinthio's principles were in the main an adaptation of Seneca's, or rather of what he took to be Seneca's purposes, to the immediate needs of Cinthio's contemporary theatre. His own object he declared to be "servire l'età, à gli spettatori." Tragedy must grip its audience. It must therefore reflect a range of experience and base itself on a system of values which are felt by its audience to be real. Many of his proposals are the direct outcome of this general principle, and one or two of them are especially pertinent to our argument. For instance, tragedy must no longer rely mainly for its material on ancient mythology nor on accredited history; for these depict a world which may have lost urgent contact with a modern audience's sense of life. The best plots for modern tragedy will be found in modern fiction. For modern fiction is the mythology of to-day. It is the corpus of story through which the world appears as it seems to be to living men; it mirrors accepted codes of conduct, displays the particular manner of contemporary consciousness, and adopts the current assumptions of human values. Let the dramatist, therefore, draw his plots from the novelists. An inevitable consequence followed from this. There is nothing in which the out-

---

"Shakespeare's Experimental Tragedy" [*Editor's title*]. From Shakespearian Tragedy *by H. B. Charlton (Cambridge, England: Cambridge University Press, 1948), pp. 49–63. Reprinted, with a brief deletion from page 61, and retitled by permission of the publisher and Mrs. Charlton.*

[1] See H. B. Charlton, Senecan Tradition in Renaissance Tragedy, first published in 1921 as an introduction to *The Poetical Works of Sir William Alexander* (Manchester University Press and Scottish Texts Society) and reissued separately by the Manchester University Press in 1946.

look on life adopted by the modern world is more different from that
of the ancient classical world than in its apprehension of the human
and spiritual significance of the love of man for woman. Love had
become for the modern world its most engrossing interest and often
its supreme experience. Modern fiction turns almost exclusively on
love. So when dramatists took their tales from the novelists, they took
love over as the main theme of their plays. Seven of Cinthio's nine
plays borrow their plots from novels (most of them from his own series,
the *Hecatommithi*); the other two are "classical," but are two of the
great classical love stories, *Dido* and *Cleopatra*. Jason de Nores, a much
more conservatively Aristotelian expositor than his contemporary
Cinthio, to exemplify the form which the most perfect tragedy could
take, constructs the plot for it from one of Boccaccio's tales.

Whether by direct influence or by mere force of circumstance,
Cinthio's practice prevailed. Sixteen-century tragedy found rich material in the novels. But the traditionalists were perpetually reminding
the innovators that tragedy always had had and always must have an
historical hero. "In tragoedia reges, principes, ex urbibus, arcibus,
castris," Scaliger, the Parnassian legislator, announced. No one would
accept a hero as great unless his memory were preserved in the his-
torian's pages. "C'est l'histoire qui persuade avec empire," as Corneille
put it. Shakespeare, an eager and humble apprentice, naturally followed traditional custom. *Titus Andronicus, Richard III* and *Richard
II* belong in the main to the conventional pattern. They deal with
historical material. Their heroes are of high rank and potent in deter-
mining the destiny of nations. The plot is never mainly a lovers' story,
though a love-intrigue intrudes sporadically here and there within the
major theme. But somehow the prescriptions had not produced the
expected result. There was something unsatisfying in these plays as
divinations of man's tragic lot. And so the conventions were jettisoned
in *Romeo and Juliet*.

Shakespeare was casting in fresh directions to find the universality,
the momentousness, and above all the inevitability of all-compelling
tragedy. In particular, he was experimenting with a new propelling
force, a new final sanction as the determinant energy, the *ultima ratio*
of tragedy's inner world; and though *Romeo and Juliet* is set in a
modern Christian country, with church and priest and full ecclesiastical
institution, the whole universe of God's justice, vengeance and providence is discarded and rejected from the directing forces of the play's
dramatic movement. In its place, there is a theatrical resuscitation of
the half-barbarian, half-Roman deities of Fate and Fortune.

The plot of *Romeo and Juliet* is pure fiction. Shakespeare took it from Arthur Brooke's poem, *The Tragicall Historie of Romeus and Juliet* (1562). Shakespeare knew from Brooke's title-page that the tale was taken from an Italian novelist, "written first in Italian by Bandell." He knew, too, what sort of novels Bandello wrote, for Painter had retold them in his *Palace of Pleasure* (1567). They were clear fictions. Moreover the hero and the heroine, Romeo and Juliet, had none of the pomp of historic circumstance about them; they were socially of the minor aristocracy who were to stock Shakespeare's comedies, and their only political significance was an adventitious rôle in the civic disturbance of a small city-state. Romeo and Juliet were in effect just a boy and a girl in a novel; and as such they had no claim to the world's attention except through their passion and their fate.

To choose such folk as these for tragic heroes was aesthetically well-nigh an anarchist's gesture; and the dramatist provided a sort of programme-prologue to prompt the audience to see the play from the right point of view. In this play-bill the dramatist draws special attention to two features of his story. First, Verona was being torn by a terrible, bloodthirsty feud which no human endeavour had been able to settle; this was the direct cause of the death of the lovers, and but for those deaths it never would have been healed. Second, the course of the young lovers' lives is from the outset governed by a malignant destiny; fatal, star-crossed, death-marked, they are doomed to piteous destruction.

The intent of this emphasis is clear. The tale will end with the death of two ravishingly attractive young folk; and the dramatist must exonerate himself from all complicity in their murder, lest he be found guilty of pandering to a liking for a human shambles. He disowns responsibility and throws it on Destiny, Fate. The device is well warranted in the tragic tradition, and especially in its Senecan models. But whether, in fact, it succeeds is a matter for further consideration. The invocation of Fate is strengthened by the second feature scored heavily in the prologue, the feud. The feud is, so to speak, the means by which Fate acts. The feud is to provide the sense of immediate, and Fate that of ultimate, inevitability. For it may happen that, however the dramatist deploys his imaginative suggestions, he may fail to summon up a Fate sufficiently compelling to force itself upon the audience as unquestioned shaper of the tragic end. In such circumstance Romeo's and Juliet's death would be by mere chance, a gratuitous intervention by a dramatist exercising his homicidal proclivities for the joy of his audience. Hence the feud has a further function. It will be the dramatist's last plea for exculpation or for mercy; and it will allow his audience to absolve him or to forgive him without loss of its own

"philanthropy"; for through death came the healing of the feud, and
with it, the removal of the threat to so many other lives.

It becomes, therefore, of critical importance to watch Shakespeare's
handling of these two motives, Fate and Feud, to see how he fits them
to fulfil their function, and to ask how far in fact they are adequate to
the rôle they must perforce play. Both Fate and Feud, although absent
as motives from the earliest European form of the Romeo and Juliet
story, had grown variously in the successive tellings of the tale before
it came to Brooke.[2] The general trend had been to magnify the viru-
lence of the feud, and, even more notably, to swell the sententious
apostrophising of Fate's malignity. Brooke, for instance, misses no
opportunity for such sententiousness. Longer or shorter, there are at
least fifteen passages in his poem where the malignity of Fate is his
conventionally poetic theme. "Froward fortune," "fortune's cruel will,"
"wavering fortune," "tickel fortune," "when fortune list to strike,"
"false fortune cast for her, poore wretch, a myschiefe newe to brewe,"
"dame fortune did assent," "with piteous plaint, fierce fortune doth he
blame," "till Attropos shall cut my fatall thread of lyfe," "though cruel
fortune be so much my dedly foe," "the blyndfyld goddesse that with
frowning face doth fraye, and from theyr seate the mighty kinges
throwes downe with hedlong sway," "He cryed out, with open mouth,
against the starres above, The fatall sisters three, he said, had done
him wrong"—so, again and again, does Brooke bring in

> The diversenes, and eke the accidents so straunge,
> Of frayle unconstant Fortune, that delyteth still in chaunge.[3]

Romeo cries aloud

> Against the restles starres, in rolling skyes that raunge,
> Against the fatall sisters three, and Fortune full of chaunge.[4]

There are more elaborate set speeches on the same theme:

> For Fortune chaungeth more, than fickel fantasie;
> In nothing Fortune constant is, save in unconstancie.
> Her hasty ronning wheele, is of a restles coorse,

---

[2] For differences between the many pre-Shakespearian versions, see H. B. Charlton,
Romeo and Juliet as an Experimental Tragedy (British Academy Shakespeare
Lecture, 1939) and "France as Chaperone of Romeo and Juliet" in *Studies in French
presented to M. K. Pope*, Manchester University Press (1939).

[3] Brooke, *Romeus and Juliet* (Hazlitt's Shakespeare's Library, vol. 1. 1875), p. 142.

[4] *Ibid.* p. 151.

That turnes the clymers hedlong downe, from better to the woorse,
And those that are beneth, she heaveth up agayne.[5]

So when Shakespeare took up the story, Brooke had already sought to drench it in fatality. But since Shakespeare was a dramatist, he could not handle Fate and Feud as could a narrative poet. His feud will enter, not descriptively, but as action; and for fate he must depend on the sentiments of his characters and on an atmosphere generated by the sweep of the action. The feud may be deferred for a moment to watch Shakespeare's handling of Fate.

His most frequent device is to adapt what Brooke's practice had been; instead of letting his persons declaim formally, as Brooke's do, against the inconstancy of Fortune, he endows them with dramatic premonitions. Setting out for Capulet's ball, Romeo is suddenly sad:

> my mind misgives
> Some consequence, yet hanging in the stars,
> Shall bitterly begin his fearful date
> With this night's revels; and expire the term
> Of a despised life, clos'd in my breast,
> By some vile forfeit of untimely death:
> But he that hath the steerage of my course
> Direct my sail![6]

As the lovers first declare their passion, Juliet begs Romeo not to swear, as if an oath might be an evil omen:

> I have no joy of this contract to-night:
> It is too rash, too unadvised, too sudden;
> Too like the lightning, which doth cease to be
> Ere one can say "It lightens." [7]

Romeo, involved in the fatal fight, cries "O, I am fortune's fool!" [8] Looking down from her window at Romeo as he goes into exile, Juliet murmurs

> O God, I have an ill-divining soul!
> Methinks I see thee, now thou art below,
> As one dead in the bottom of a tomb.[9]

---

[5] Brooke, *Romeus and Juliet* (Hazlitt's Shakespeare's Library, vol. I. 1875), p. 147. See also pp. 97, 115.
[6] *Romeo and Juliet* I. iv. 106. [8] *Ibid.* III. i. 141.
[7] *Ibid.* II. ii. 117. [9] *Ibid.* III. v. 54.

With dramatic irony Juliet implores her parents to defer her marriage with Paris:

> Or, if you do not, make the bridal bed
> In that dim monument where Tybalt lies.[10]

Besides these promptings of impending doom there are premonitions of a less direct kind. The friar fears the violence of the lover's passion:

> These violent delights have violent ends
> And in their triumph die, like fire and powder,
> Which as they kiss consume.[11]

Another source of omen in the play is the presaging of dreams; for from the beginning of time, "the world of sleep, the realm of wild reality" has brought dreams which look like heralds of eternity and speak like Sybils of the future. There is much dreaming in *Romeo and Juliet*. Mercutio may mock at dreams as children of an idle brain, begot of nothing but vain phantasy. But when Romeo says he "dream'd a dream to-night," Mercutio's famous flight of fancy recalls the universal belief in dreams as foreshadowings of the future. Again Romeo dreams; this time, "I dreamt my lady came and found me dead." [12] As his man Balthasar waits outside Juliet's tomb, he dreams that his master and another are fighting and the audience knows how accurately the dream mirrors the true facts.

But Shakespeare not only hangs omens thickly round his play. He gives to the action itself a quality apt to conjure the sense of relentless doom. It springs mainly from his compression of the time over which the story stretches. In all earlier versions there is a much longer lapse. Romeo's wooing is prolonged over weeks before the secret wedding; then, after the wedding, there is an interval of three or four months before the slaying of Tybalt; and Romeo's exile lasts from Easter until a short time before mid-September when the marriage with Paris was at first planned to take place. But in Shakespeare all this is pressed into three or four days. The world seems for a moment to be caught up in the fierce play of furies revelling in some mad supernatural game.

But before asking whether the sense of an all-controlling Fate is made strong enough to fulfil its tragic purpose let us turn to the feud. Here Shakespeare's difficulties are even greater. Italian novelists of the quattro- or cinquecento, throwing their story back through two or

[10] *Ibid.* iii. v. 202.   [12] *Ibid.* v. i. 6.
[11] *Ibid.* ii. vi. 9.

three generations, might expect their readers easily to accept a fierce vendetta. But the Verona which Shakespeare depicts is a highly civilised world, with an intellectual and artistic culture and an implied social attainment altogether alien from the sort of society in which a feud is a more or less natural manifestation of enmity. The border country of civilisation is the home of feuds, a region where social organisation is still of the clan, where the head of the family-clan is a strong despot, and where law has not progressed beyond the sort of wild justice of which one instrument is the feud.

> For ere I cross the border fells,
> The tane of us shall die

It was wellnigh impossible for Shakespeare to fit the bloodlust of a border feud into the social setting of his Verona. The heads of the rival houses are not at all the fierce chieftains who rule with ruthless despotism. When old Capulet, in fire-side gown, bustles to the scene of the fray and calls for his sword, his wife tells him bluntly that it is a crutch which an old man such as he should want, and not a weapon. Montague, too, spits a little verbal fire, but his wife plucks him by the arm, and tells him to calm down: "thou shalt not stir one foot to seek a foe." Indeed, these old men are almost comic figures, and especially Capulet. His querulous fussiness, his casual bonhomie, his almost senile humour and his childish irascibility hardly make him the pattern of a clan chieftain. Even his domestics put him in his place:

> Go, you cot-quean, go,
> Get you to bed; faith, you'll be sick to-morrow
> For this night's watching,[13]

the Nurse tells him; and the picture is filled in by his wife's reminder that she has put a stop to his "mouse-hunting." There is of course the prince's word that

> Three civil brawls, bred of an airy word,
> By thee, old Capulet, and Montague,
> Have thrice disturb'd the quiet of our streets.[14]

But these brawls bred of an airy word are no manifestations of a really ungovernable feud. When Montague and Capulet are bound by the prince to keep the peace, old Capulet himself says

> 'tis not hard, I think,
> For men so old as we to keep the peace.[15]

---

[13] *Romeo and Juliet* IV. iv. 7.   [15] *Ibid.* I. ii. 2.
[14] *Ibid.* I. i. 96.

and there is a general feeling that the old quarrel has run its course. Paris, suitor to Juliet, says it is a pity that the Capulets and the Montagues have lived at odds so long. And Benvolio, a relative of the Montagues, is a consistent peace-maker. He tries to suppress a brawl amongst the rival retainers, and invites Tybalt, a Capulet, to assist him in the work. Later he begs his friends to avoid trouble by keeping out of the way of the Capulets, for it is the season of hot blood:

> I pray thee, good Mercutio, let's retire:
> The day is hot, the Capulets abroad,
> And if we meet, we shall not scape a brawl;
> For now, these hot days, is the mad blood stirring.[16]

When the hot-blooded Mercutio does incite Tybalt to a quarrel, it is again Benvolio who tries to preserve the peace:

> We talk here in the public haunt of men:
> Either withdraw unto some private place,
> And reason coldly of your grievances,
> Or else depart.[17]

Hence the jest of Mercutio's famous description of Benvolio as an inveterate quarreller, thirsting for the slightest excuse to draw sword.

Moreover, the rival houses have mutual friends. Mercutio, Montague Romeo's close acquaintance, is an invited guest at the Capulets' ball. Stranger still, so is Romeo's cruel lady, Rosaline, who in the invitation is addressed as Capulet's cousin. It is odd that Romeo's love for her, since she was a Capulet, had given him no qualms on the score of the feud. When Romeo is persuaded to go gate-crashing to the ball because Rosaline will be there, there is no talk at all of its being a hazardous undertaking. Safety will require, if even so much, no more than a mask.[18] On the way to the ball, as talk is running gaily, there is still no mention of danger involved. Indeed, the feud is almost a dead letter so far. The son of the Montague does not know what the Capulet daughter looks like, nor she what he is like. The traditional hatred survives only in one or two high-spirited, hot-blooded scions on either side, and in the kitchen-folk. Tybalt alone

---

[16] *Ibid.* III. i. 1.   [17] *Romeo and Juliet* III. i. 53.
[18] In the earlier versions the mask is not a precaution for safety. Shakespeare, taking it partly as such, has to realise how utterly ineffective it is. Romeo is soon known:

> This, by his voice, should be a Montague!
> Fetch me my rapier, boy. What dares the slave
> Come hither, cover'd with an antic face,
> To flee and scorn at our solemnity?   (I. v. 56.)

resents Romeo's presence at the ball, yet it is easy for all to recognise him; and because Tybalt feels Romeo's coming to be an insult, he seeks him out next day to challenge him, so providing the immediate occasion of the new outburst. Naturally, once blood is roused again, and murder done, the ancient rancour springs up with new life. Even Lady Capulet has comically Machiavellian plans for having Romeo poisoned in Mantua. But prior to this the evidences of the feud are so unsubstantial that the forebodings of Romeo and Juliet, discovering each other's name, seem prompted more by fate than feud. There will, of course, be family difficulties; but the friar marries them without a hesitating qualm, feeling that such a union is bound to be accepted eventually by the parents, who will thus be brought to amity.

The most remarkable episode, however, is still to be named. When Tybalt discovers Romeo at the ball, infuriated he rushes to Capulet with the news. But Capulet, in his festive mood, is pleasantly interested, saying that Romeo is reputed to be good-looking and quite a pleasant boy. He tells Tybalt to calm himself, to remember his manners, and to treat Romeo properly:

> Content thee, gentle coz, let him alone;
> He bears him like a portly gentleman;
> And, to say truth, Verona brags of him
> To be a virtuous and well govern'd youth:
> I would not for the wealth of all the town
> Here in my house do him disparagement:
> Therefore be patient, take no note of him:
> It is my will, the which if thou respect,
> Show a fair presence and put off these frowns,
> An ill-beseeming semblance for a feast.[19]

When Tybalt is reluctant, old Capulet is annoyed and testily tells him to stop being a saucy youngster:

> He shall be endured:
> What, goodman boy! I say, he shall: go to.
> Am I the master here or you? Go to.
> You'll not endure him! God shall mend my soul!
> You'll make a mutiny among my guests!
> You will set cock-a-hoop! You'll be the man!
> . . . Go to, go to;
> You are a saucy boy: is't so indeed?
> This trick may chance to scathe you, I know what:

[19] *Romeo and Juliet* I. v. 67.

> You must contrary me! marry, 'tis time.
> Well said, my hearts! You are a princox; go.[20]

This is a scene which sticks in the memory; for here the dramatist, unencumbered by a story, is interpolating a lively scene in his own kind, a vignette of two very amusing people in an amusing situation. But it is unfortunate for the feud that this episode takes so well. For clearly old Capulet is unwilling to let the feud interrupt a dance; and a quarrel which is of less moment than a galliard is being appeased at an extravagant price, if the price is the death of two such delightful creatures as Romeo and Juliet;

> their parents' rage,
> Which, but their children's end, naught could remove,[21]

loses all its plausibility. A feud like this will not serve as the bribe it was meant to be; it is no atonement for the death of the lovers. Nor, indeed, is it coherent and impressive enough as part of the plot to propel the sweep of necessity in the sequence of events. If the tragedy is to march relentlessly to its end, leaving no flaw in the sense of inevitability which it seeks to prompt, it clearly must depend for that indispensable tragic impression not on its feud, but on its scattered suggestions of doom and of malignant fate. And, as has been seen, Shakespeare harps frequently on this theme.

But how far can a Roman sense of Fate be made real for a modern audience? It is no mere matter of exciting thought to "wander through eternity" in the wake of the mystery which surrounds the human lot. Mystery must take on positive shape, and half-lose itself in dread figures controlling human life in their malice. The forms and the phrases by which these powers had been invoked were a traditional part in the inheritance of the Senecan drama which came to sixteenth-century Europe. Fortuna, Fatum, Fata, Parcae: all were firmly established in its *dramatis personae*. . . .

But with what conviction could a sixteenth-century spectator take over these ancient figures? Even the human beings of an old mythology may lose their compelling power; "what's Hecuba to him, or he to Hecuba?" But the gods are in a much worse case; pagan, they had faded before the God of the Christians: *Vicisti, Galilæe!* Fate was no longer a deity strong enough to carry the responsibility of a tragic universe; at most, it could intervene casually as pure luck, and bad luck as a motive turns tragedy to mere chance. It lacks entirely the

---

[20] *Romeo and Juliet* I. v. 78.
[21] *Ibid.* Prologue, l. II.

ultimate tragic ἀνάγκη [necessity]. It fails to provide the indispensable inevitability.

Is then Shakespeare's *Romeo and Juliet* an unsuccessful experiment? To say so may seem not only profane but foolish. In its own day, as the dog's-eared Bodley Folio shows, and ever since, it has been one of Shakespeare's most preferred plays. It is indeed rich in spells of its own. But as a pattern of the idea of tragedy, it is a failure. Even Shakespeare appears to have felt that, as an experiment, it had disappointed him. At all events, he abandoned tragedy for the next few years and gave himself to history and to comedy; and even afterwards, he fought shy of the simple theme of love, and of the love of anybody less than a great political figure as the main matter for his tragedies.

Nevertheless it is obvious that neither sadism nor masochism is remotely conscious in our appreciation of *Romeo and Juliet,* nor is our "philanthropy" offended by it. But the achievement is due to the magic of Shakespeare's poetic genius and to the intermittent force of his dramatic power rather than to his grasp of the foundations of tragedy.

There is no need here to follow the meetings of Romeo and Juliet through the play, and to recall the spell of Shakespeare's poetry as it transports us along the rushing stream of the lovers' passion, from its sudden outbreak to its consummation in death. Romeo seals his "dateless bargain to engrossing death," choosing shipwreck on the dashing rocks to secure peace for his "sea-sick weary bark." Juliet has but a word: "I'll be brief. O happy dagger!" There is need for nothing beyond this. Shakespeare, divining their naked passion, lifts them above the world and out of life by the mere force of it. It is the sheer might of poetry. Dramatically, however, he has subsidiary resources. He has Mercutio and the Nurse.

Shakespeare's Mercutio has the gay poise and the rippling wit of the man of the world. By temperament he is irrepressible and merry; his charm is infectious. His speech runs freely between fancies of exquisite delicacy and the coarser fringe of worldly humour; and he has the sensitiveness of sympathetic fellowship. Such a man, if any at all, might have understood the depth of Romeo's love for Juliet. But the *camaraderie* and the worldly *savoir-faire* of Mercutio give him no inkling of the nature of Romeo's passion. The love of Romeo and Juliet is beyond the ken of their friends; it belongs to a world which is not their world; and so the passing of Romeo and Juliet is not as other deaths are in their impact on our sentiments.

Similarly, too, the Nurse. She is Shakespeare's greatest debt to Brooke, in whose poem she plays a curiously unexpected and yet incongruously entertaining part. She is the one great addition which

Brooke made to the saga. She is garrulous, worldly, coarse, vulgar, and babblingly given to reminiscence stuffed with native animal humour and self-assurance. Shakespeare gladly borrowed her, and so gave his Juliet for her most intimate domestic companion a gross worldly creature who talks much of love and never means anything beyond sensuality. Like Romeo's, Juliet's love is completely unintelligible to the people in her familiar circle. To her nurse, love is animal lust. To her father, who has been a "mouse-hunter" in his time, and to her mother, it is merely a social institution, a worldly arrangement in a very worldly world. This earth, it would seem, has no place for passion like Romeo's and Juliet's. And so, stirred to sympathy by Shakespeare's poetic power, we tolerate, perhaps even approve, their death. At least for the moment.

But tragedy lives not only for its own moment, nor by long "suspensions of disbelief." There is the inevitable afterthought and all its "obstinate questionings." Our sentiments were but momentarily gratified. And finally our deeper consciousness protests. Shakespeare has but conquered us by a trick: the experiment carries him no nearer to the heart of tragedy.

Light Images in *Romeo and Juliet*

by Caroline F. E. Spurgeon

In *Romeo and Juliet* the beauty and ardour of young love are seen by Shakespeare as the irradiating glory of sunlight and starlight in a dark world. The dominating image is *light*, every form and manifestation of it: the sun, moon, stars, fire, lightning, the flash of gunpowder, and the reflected light of beauty and of love; while by contrast we have night, darkness, clouds, rain, mist and smoke.

Each of the lovers thinks of the other as light; Romeo's overpowering impression when he first catches sight of Juliet on the fateful evening at the Capulets' ball is seen in his exclamation,

> O, she doth teach the torches to burn bright!
> It seems she hangs upon the cheek of night
> Like a rich jewel in an Ethiop's ear.

To Juliet, Romeo is "day in night"; to Romeo, Juliet is the sun rising from the east, and when they soar to love's ecstasy, each alike pictures the other as stars in heaven, shedding such brightness as puts to shame the heavenly bodies themselves.

The intensity of feeling in both lovers purges even the most highly affected and euphuistic conceits of their artificiality, and transforms them into the exquisite and passionate expression of love's rhapsody.

Thus Romeo plays with the old conceit that two of the fairest stars in heaven, having some business on earth, have entreated Juliet's eyes to take their place till they return, and he conjectures,

> What if her eyes were there, they in her head?

If so,

> The brightness of her cheek would shame those stars,
> As daylight doth a lamp;

"Light Images in Romeo and Juliet." *From* Shakespeare's Imagery and What It Tells Us *by Caroline F. E. Spurgeon (Cambridge, England: Cambridge University Press, 1935), pp. 310–16. Reprinted by permission of the publisher.*

and then comes the rush of feeling, the overpowering realisation and immortal expression of the transforming glory of love:

> her eyes in heaven
> Would through the airy region stream so bright
> That birds would sing and think it were not night.

And Juliet, in her invocation to night, using an even more extravagant conceit, such as Cowley or Cleveland at his wildest never exceeded, transmutes it into the perfect and natural expression of a girl whose lover to her not only radiates light, but is, indeed, very light itself:

> Give me my Romeo; and, when he shall die,
> Take him and cut him out in little stars,
> And he will make the face of heaven so fine,
> That all the world will be in love with night,
> And pay no worship to the garish sun.

Love is described by Romeo, before he knows what it really is, as

> a smoke raised with the fume of sighs;
> Being purged, a fire sparkling in lovers' eyes;

and the messengers of love are pictured by Juliet, when she is chafing under the nurse's delay, as one of the most exquisite effects in nature, seen especially on the English hills in spring—the swift, magical, transforming power of light:

> love's heralds [she cries] should be thoughts,
> Which ten times faster glide than the sun's beams,
> Driving back shadows over louring hills.

The irradiating quality of the beauty of love is noticed by both lovers; by Juliet, in her first ecstasy, when she declares that lovers' "own beauties" are sufficient light for them to see by, and, at the end, by Romeo, when, thinking her dead, he gazes on her and cries,

> her beauty makes
> This vault a feasting presence full of light.

There can be no question, I think, that Shakespeare saw the story, in its swift and tragic beauty, as an almost blinding flash of light, suddenly ignited, and as swiftly quenched. He quite deliberately compresses the action from over nine months to the almost incredibly short period of five days; so that the lovers meet on Sunday, are wedded on Monday, part at dawn on Tuesday and are reunited in

death on the night of Thursday. The sensation of swiftness and brilliance, accompanied by danger and destruction, is accentuated again
and again; by Juliet, when she avows their betrothal

> is too rash, too unadvised, too sudden,
> Too like the lightning, which doth cease to be
> Ere one can say "It lightens";

and by Romeo and the friar, who instinctively make repeated use of
the image of the quick destructive flash of gunpowder. Indeed the
friar, in his well-known answer to Romeo's prayer for instant marriage,
succinctly, in the last nine words, sums up the whole movement of the
play:

> These violent delights have violent ends,
> And in their triumph die; like fire and powder
> Which as they kiss consume.

Even old Capulet, whom one does not think of as a poetical person,
though he uses many images—some of great beauty—carries on the
idea of light to represent love and youth and beauty, and of the
clouding of the sun for grief and sorrow. He promises Paris that on
the evening of the ball he shall see at his house

> Earth-treading stars that make dark heaven light;

and when he encounters Juliet weeping, as he thinks, for her cousin
Tybalt's death, he clothes his comment in similar nature imagery of
light quenched in darkness:

> When the sun sets, the air doth drizzle dew;
> But for the sunset of my brother's son
> It rains downright.

In addition to this more definite symbolic imagery, we find that
radiant light, sunshine, starlight, moonbeams, sunrise and sunset, the
sparkle of fire, a meteor, candles, torches, quick-coming darkness,
clouds, mist, rain and night, form a pictorial background, or running
accompaniment, to the play, which augments unconsciously in us this
same sensation.

We meet it at once in the prince's description of the attitude of the
rival houses

> That quench the fire of your pernicious rage
> With purple fountains issuing from your veins;

and later, in the talk of Benvolio and Montague about the rising sun, the dew and clouds, followed by Romeo's definition of love, Capulet's words just quoted, Benvolio's riming proverb about fire, the talk of Romeo and Mercutio about torches, candles, lights and lamps, the flashing lights and torches of the ball, four times accentuated, Romeo's conception of Juliet as a "bright angel,"

> As glorious to this night, ...
> As is a winged messenger of heaven;

in the moonlight in the orchard, the sunrise Friar Lawrence watches from his cell, the sun clearing from heaven Romeo's sighs, the exquisite light and shadow swiftly chasing over Juliet's words in the orchard, the "black fate" of the day on which Mercutio was killed, the "fire-eyed fury" which leads Romeo to challenge Tybalt, their fight, to which they go "like lightning," the sunset which Juliet so ardently desires to be swift "and bring in cloudy night immediately," the exquisite play of quivering light from darkness through dawn, till

> jocund day
> Stands tiptoe on the misty mountain tops,

which forms the theme of the lovers' parting song; and, at the last, in Romeo's anguished reply to Juliet, pointing the contrast between the coming day and their own great sorrow:

> More light and light: more dark and dark our woes!

And then, at the end, we see the darkness of the churchyard, lit by the glittering torch of Paris, quickly quenched; Romeo's arrival with his torch, the swift fight and death, the dark vault, which is not a grave but a lantern irradiated by Juliet's beauty, Romeo's grim jest on the "lightning before death," followed immediately by the self-slaughter of the "star-crossed" lovers, the gathering together of the stricken mourners as the day breaks, and the "glooming" peace of the overcast morning when

> The sun for sorrow will not show his head.

Shakespeare's extraordinary susceptibility to suggestion and readiness to borrow are well exemplified in this running imagery. He took the idea from the last place we should expect, from the wooden doggerel of Arthur Brooke, and the germ of it is in the sing-song line in which Brooke describes the attitude of the lovers:

> For each of them to other is as to the world the sun.

Their mutual feeling and the feud of the families are cor
referred to by Brooke as "fire" or "flame"; in the beginning, he
of the feud as a "mighty fire"; the families "bathe in blood of smarting wounds," and the prince hopes he may "quench the sparks that
burned within their breast." These three images are combined and
unified by Shakespeare in the two lines already quoted (p. 313). [p. 63
in this volume]

Other suggestions also come from Brooke, such as the emphasis on
the bright light of the torches at the ball; Romeo's first sight of Juliet,
which is a "sudden kindled fire"; her first impression of him, when he

> in her sight did seem to pass the rest as far
> As Phoebus' shining beams do pass the brightness of a star;

and his description in his first talk to her, of the

> quick sparks and glowing furious glead
> . . . from your beauty's pleasant eyne, Love causèd to proceed
> Which have so set on fire each feeling part of mine
> That lo, my mind doth melt away, my outward parts do pine,

which is transmuted by Shakespeare to the delightful image of the
stars which have changed places with her eyes.

But although Shakespeare took the idea from his original, it scarcely
needs saying that in taking it, he has transformed a few conventional
and obvious similes of little poetic worth into a continuous and consistent running image of exquisite beauty, building up a definite picture and atmosphere of brilliance swiftly quenched, which powerfully
affects the imagination of the reader.

Romeo and Juliet

by W. H. Clemen

In Shakespeare's work, conventional style and a freer, more spontaneous mode of expression are not opposite poles which may be definitely assigned to different periods. It is impossible to say that with a certain play, the conventional style comes to an end, and that from then on, a new style exclusively prevails. There are many transitions and interrelationships, and in some plays which stand at the turning-point between the young and the mature Shakespeare, the most traditional and conventional wording is to be found together with a direct and surprising new language which allows us to divine the Shakespeare of the great tragedies. *Romeo and Juliet* is the best example of this co-existence of two styles. H. Granville-Barker has shown how both in separate scenes and in the dramatic structure a new spontaneity often breaks through the conventional vestment, but is still not yet strong enough to pervade the whole of the play. The same thing may now be shown to hold for the imagery as well.

Many examples of the old conventional type can be selected. In the third act, Capulet finds Juliet in tears:

> How now! a conduit, girl? what, still in tears?
> Evermore showering? in one little body
> Thou counterfeit'st a bark, a sea, a wind;
> For still thy eyes, which I may call the sea,
> Do ebb and flow with tears; the bark thy body is,
> Sailing in this salt flood; the winds, thy sighs;
> Who, raging with thy tears, and they with them,
> Without a sudden calm, will overset
> Thy tempest-tossed body.   (III. v. 130)

"Romeo and Juliet." *From* The Development of Shakespeare's Imagery *by W. H. Clemen (London: Methuen & Company, Ltd.; Cambridge, Mass.: Harvard University Press, 1951), pp. 63–73. Copyright 1951 by Methuen & Company, Ltd. Reprinted by permission of the publishers.*

This image still presents all the features of Shakespeare's early style
—the vain pleasure taken in painting every detail of the little picture
whose fastidious construction recalls the conceits of the early comedies.
The situation, too, in which the father finds his daughter dissolved in
tears, seems to us unsuitable for such an elaborate comparison. Of
course, tears are often the occasion for an image. But, for example,
when Richard III says to his mother, "The liquid drops of tears that
you have shed shall come again, transform'd to orient pearl" (iv. iv.
321), the figurative phrase is meant to lend the whole chain of thought
a greater force; Richard *intends* to express something by it. Capulet,
on the other hand, pursues no aim with this image; the occasion is
merely the excuse for the image. Expressions such as "thou counter-
feit'st" or "which I may call the sea," as well as the agglomeration of
words, betray the pleasure of invention. However, this artificiality and
the very circumstantiality of this mode of expression is itself highly
fitting for Juliet's verbose and conventional father, for his affability
and vain self-admiration (cf. his simile with the "well-apparell'd
April" at i. ii. 27). Thus this passage characterizes Capulet. A stylistic
form belonging to Shakespeare's earliest period is here fitted into a
place that suits it. This we may observe at many points in *Romeo and
Juliet*. Brother Lorenzo is characterized in a similar way by his sententious and pedantic images, by the leisurely breadth of his flowery and
often descriptive manner of speech.

On the whole it may be said, that the first scenes of *Romeo and
Juliet* strike us as being more conventional in tone and diction than
the later ones. The blank-verse, too, is handled more conventionally
here than in the later parts of the play. It may very well be that this
is intentional.[1] For the nearer the play advances towards its tragic
culmination, the less powerful and significant becomes the conventional world from which the two lovers have freed themselves by
accepting their fate. This transition of style has not, of course, been
worked out consistently. The rhetoric and the declamatory style never
quite vanish, and are certainly not meant to disappear entirely. Their
persistence, however, may set off better those passages (more frequent
in the last acts), in which we find a new simplicity and poignant
directness of diction, as in Romeo's famous line, "Is it even so? Then
I defy you, stars!" (v. i. 24). This manner of placing significant moments and passages into fuller relief, by contrasting them with very
different stylistic patterns has been most effectively used by Shake-

[1] This surmise is also expressed by T. S. Eliot in a lecture given in Germany on
"The Development of Shakespeare's Versification" published in German under the
title "Shakespeares Verskunst," *Der Monat, II*, [no.] 20, [May] 1950, [198–207].

speare throughout the whole play.[2] It is interesting to trace this art of contrast in the use of imagery; it accounts not only for many subtle dramatic effects, but also for several juxtapositions which appear odd at first sight, but become clear when judged from the context.

That the same characters speak in this play, now in a very conventional, now in quite a new and different manner, may best be seen with Romeo. It is he who (besides Juliet and the nurse) is most often able to rise above the level of flowery or witty, conventional phrase (as in the balcony scene and in the garden scene). But, on the other hand, he is just as much confined to this conventional mode as all the others. If we look closer, however, we see that this change in diction in Romeo is not the result of chance but rather of a change in his mood.[3] Before Romeo has met Juliet, he still finds pleasure in polished and witty dialogue with Benvolio, speaks of "love" in the usual stereotyped phrases, using in his speech, apart from metaphors, a great variety of other figures which contribute to the artificiality of his whole utterance at this stage of the play.[4]

> Love is a smoke raised with the fume of sighs;
> Being purged, a fire sparkling in lovers' eyes;
> Being vex'd, a sea nourish'd with lovers' tears: (I. i. 196)

and thus, in a similar dialogue which he—also in the first act—holds with Mercutio, he cleverly and gracefully catches up the image of Cupid's wings tossed to him by Mercutio and proceeds to dwell upon it artfully (I. iv. 17). He meets Juliet for the first time at the feast in the house of Capulet (I. v.), and the image, with which their first conversation opens, is almost too well known to be quoted:

> *Romeo.* My lips, two blushing pilgrims, ready stand
> To smooth that rough touch with a tender kiss.

[2] For this aspect cf. H. Granville-Barker, *Prefaces to Shakespeare,* 2nd series, 1930 (*Romeo and Juliet*). [The bulk of this essay appears as the first selection in this volume—ED.]

[3] E. K. Chambers: "Romeo has been an amorist, posing before the mirror of his own self-consciousness, with tears and sighs and early morning walks and an affectation of solitude and the humorous night. He was for the numbers that Petrarch flowed in, has rhymed love and dove, and nick-named Cupid with paradox and artful phrases . . ." (*Shakespeare, A Survey* [London: Sidgwick & Jackson, Ltd., 1925], p. 71).

[4] In an illuminating article on "Patterns of Style in *Romeo and Juliet*" (*Studia Neophilologica, XXI* [(1948/49), 195–210]), J. W. Draper traces the distribution of figures and their adaptation to plot and character. Analysing the first scene he points out that the wealth of figures in Romeo's language gives to his speech "a witty artificiality that suggests that his pangs of love are not too deep" (p. 198).

> *Juliet.* Good pilgrim, you do wrong your hand too much,
> Which mannerly devotion shows in this;
> For saints have hands that pilgrims' hands do touch,
> And palm to palm is holy palmer's kiss.   (I. v. 97)

This passage, joined by its cross-rime, is a typical example of the balanced, symmetrical and artificial style of the early Shakespeare. In pretty and obedient fashion, this motif is elaborated in seven lines by both parties. In these formal surroundings the first meeting of the lovers must be formal, too, and is accordingly reflected in a conventional language.

But this same Romeo speaks a new language in those two scenes with Juliet, which stand out from the drama like unforgettable peaks: the garden scene and the balcony scene. Here two characters meet who no longer carry on coquetry with elegant conceits on "love" but who are passionately in love with one another and give direct expression to their love. The fact that, in *Romeo and Juliet,* Shakespeare shaped human love for the first time in *timeless* form gives this play an important position not only in his own development, but also in the history of the Elizabethan drama. This fundamental experience of deep and passionate love is at the very base of the whole drama; in these two scenes it finds its most genuine expression. For these scenes bring the secret converse of the lovers, freed from their conventional environment and from distraction, but at one with the heart of nature. The warmth and tenderness of these scenes raises the language to a poetic height and richness unmatched in Shakespeare's work and the imagery displays a complexity surpassing everything hitherto found:

> O, speak again, bright angel! for thou art
> As glorious to this night, being o'er my head,
> As is a winged messenger of heaven
> Unto the white-upturned wondering eyes
> Of mortals that fall back to gaze on him
> When he bestrides the lazy-pacing clouds
> And sails upon the bosom of the air.   (II. ii. 26)

Judged by its style, this is indeed still descriptive, meticulously handled imagery, rich in epithets. But the way this image is connected with the situation and the characters is new; it springs wholly from the situation and contains nothing extraneous, whereas up to this point, the images had been illustrated by comparisons from other spheres. Now the situation is itself of such a metaphorical nature, that it permits an organic growth of the image; Romeo stands below in the

dark garden, above which slow-sailing clouds move in a star-strewn sky
(all this is conjured up by his words!); Juliet appears above at the
window. Romeo must lift his eyes, just as one must glance upward in
order to perceive the heavenly bodies (the white-upturned eyes are his
own eyes). When, in the first lines, the eyes of the beloved appear to
Romeo as "two of the fairest stars in all the heaven," then this is no
conventional phrase but is based on the reality of the moment, on the
fact that he has raised his eyes to heaven and to Juliet at the same
time. And when Juliet now appears to him—in the image quoted—
as "winged messenger of heaven," this, too, results from the metaphorical character of the situation itself. So everything in this image has a
double function: the clouds and the heavenly *messengers* may be
reality, and at the same time they are symbols. The deeply organic
nature of this image is to be seen also in the fact that it coincides as
a poetic, enhancing element with Romeo's ecstatically uplifted mind.
Its inspiration belongs to this moment and to no other; this symbolical
moment gave Romeo's words the power to rise above the levels of
expression hitherto achieved. In this image three functions merge,
which we usually meet separately: it is the enhanced expression of
Romeo's own nature, it characterizes Juliet (light, the most important
symbol for her, occurs here), and it fills the night with clouds and stars,
thus creating atmosphere.

In this scene, it must be admitted, there are still many themes of
imagery which appear unoriginal, culled perhaps from the stock-motifs
of Elizabethan poetry. Such are the two dainty bird-images which
Juliet employs (159, 178), her asseveration "Else would I tear the cave
where Echo lies" (162) and Romeo's

> . . . wert thou as far
> As that vast shore wash'd with the farthest sea.   (82)

Still the tenderness and intensity of the feeling which pulses through
this whole scene, can occasionally permit so worn a comparison as that
of love to the deepest ocean to appear in a wording whose simple
straightforwardness[5] makes us wholly forget the conventionality of the
image, such as Juliet's:

> My bounty is as boundless as the sea,

[5] In his chapter on *Romeo and Juliet* H. Granville-Barker gives several examples
for the spontaneity of the language, which then slips back into rhetorical declamation and masterly verbosity, as, for example, Juliet's "O serpent heart, hid with a
flowering face!" (III. ii. 73) or Romeo's eloquent and conventional lament of the dead
before he takes his own life (V. iii. 83 sqq.).

My love as deep; the more I give to thee,
The more I have, for both are infinite.   (133)

The transition we perceive in *Romeo and Juliet* cannot therefore adequately be described as a transition from "conventional" to "natural" speech. For Shakespeare does not simply abandon the language of conceit or the use of artificial and highly elaborated imagery. The change lies rather in the different impression these passages make on us.[6] For they strike us as being more natural, more spontaneous. And this is due to their being more closely adapted to the situation and to the moment. They convince us because we feel the intense emotion that is expressed by them, and we now believe the characters who utter such language.

If we ask how Shakespeare in *Romeo and Juliet* tried to individualize the characters by means of imagery, we are tempted to think first of the Nurse's language. The Nurse's language, however, though the most striking example of individualized speech in Shakespeare's work of this period, is characterized less by imagery than by certain features of style, syntax and rhythm. But the contrast between Mercutio's and Romeo's language is also a contrast between their different use of imagery. The heightened lyricism of Romeo's idealizing language is set off by Mercutio's sparkling and realistic speech, which abounds in drastic comparisons, witty puns and vivid concrete pictures. In the sequence of the scenes, Shakespeare makes rich and effective use of this contrast, gay, turbulent and restless scenes being set against the more solemn and lyrical pathos of the scenes between the two lovers. The contrast in imagery, however, is developed gradually. In I. iv. Mercutio and Romeo still meet on the same level of clever word-play and conventional love-imagery. The famous Queen-Mab speech by Mercutio—though being more in the poetical than in the realistic vein[7]—shows that even in this highly imaginative passage Mercutio does not lose hold of firm reality, for a wealth of minutely observed concrete and palpable things taken from the everyday world appears in his images and comparisons. As to the difference between Romeo's and Juliet's imagery, Dr. Schmetz has drawn attention to Juliet's imagery being more tinged by the familiar objects of her life-sphere and her child-experience, whereas Romeo's imagery appears less con-

---

[6] For this process cf. John Middleton Murry, *Shakespeare*, London, 1936, Chapter XII.
[7] L. L. Schücking emphasizes that the Queen-Mab Speech is "out of character" and little consistent with Mercutio's temperament (*Character Problems in Shakespeare's Plays*, London, 1922, p. 97). For a divergent opinion cf. J. I. M. Stewart, *Character and Motive in Shakespeare*, London, 1949, p. 60.

crete and more spiritualized.[8] This subtle differentiation shows that
typical features of the character's background and mood slip into the
imagery. As with other aspects of the imagery in *Romeo and Juliet*,
however, this discrimination has not been consistently carried out. We
find a tentative beginning of Shakespeare's later technique of giving
each character his own language and imagery, but we do not find this
technique fully or consistently developed.

Nature, which plays so great a part in the garden scene and is
referred to again and again by the imagery, accompanies the whole
action of the play almost symbolically. A brief review may make clear
the advance which *Romeo and Juliet* signifies in this respect. Only
occasionally do the early comedies contain references to the time of
day and atmosphere: there is, for instance, the first line of the fifth act
of *Two Gentlemen*: "The sun begins to gild the western sky"; but in
general, these comedies are without light and we are not conscious of
the presence of nature. *Henry VI* has only two night scenes, which,
however, are introduced by fairly isolated images (namely, B [Part
Two], I. iv. and IV. i.). *Richard III* is the first play of Shakespeare's to
contain a scene—but only one scene—in which the atmosphere is
suggested by frequently interspersed references and images.[9] But such

---

[8] Thus, for Juliet, night is "a sober-suited matron" which she asks:

> Hood my unmann'd blood . . .
> With thy black mantle.
>
> (III. ii. 14)

Juliet speaks of "bud of love" (II. ii. 121) and "mansion of a love" (III. ii. 26) and
compares her impatience to that of a child "that hath new robes/And may not wear
them" (III. ii. 30). To show the more spiritual and less sensuous quality of Romeo's
imagery, Dr. Schmetz, elaborating an observation first made by Gregor Sarrazin (*Aus
Shakespeares Meisterwerkstatt, Stilgeschichtliche Studien*, Berlin, 1906) compares
Juliet's

> . . . when he shall die,
> Take him and cut him out in little stars,
> And he will make the face of heaven so fine
> That all the world will be in love with night.
>
> (III. ii. 21)

with Romeo's

> . . . her eyes in heaven
> Would through the airy region stream so bright
> That birds would sing and think it were not night.
>
> (II. ii. 20)

[9] "The weary sun hath made a golden set," etc. (V. iii. 19); "In to our tent; the air
is raw and cold" (V. iii. 46); "The silent hours steal on,/And flaky darkness breaks
within the east" (V. iii. 86); "The early village-cock/Hath twice done salutation to
the morn;" (V. iii. 210); "Who saw the sun to-day?" (V. iii. 277).

references to nature are not yet brought into harmony with the characters. Here lies the problem which faces the dramatist: all the words spoken by the characters must be the expression of themselves, must progressively reveal their nature and their mind to us. But the difficulty is now to bring in circumstances, atmosphere, historical and political explanations which are necessary for understanding and rounding off the whole, but which seem to bear relationship to no particular character. It is very illuminating to follow step by step how Shakespeare solves this problem. In the early plays, especially in the histories and in *Titus Andronicus*, Shakespeare obviously charges some figure or other in the opening scenes with the task of giving us an exhaustive description of the circumstances (the monologue is also often used for this purpose). This appears rather clumsy, and it is indeed an advance when this task is distributed among several characters. The same method, of course, now applies to the nature-images creating atmosphere. They are put into the mouths of certain characters as brief extra-dramatic digressions, they preface the events like signs (cf. *B* [Part Two] *Henry VI*, iv. i. 1). In the development of imagery, the garden scene and the balcony scene are of importance, because it is here for the first time that "nature-imagery" derives from the characters as their own expression of mood. Romeo and Juliet deliver no excursive speeches, they utter merely their own being and their love for one another, but their words reveal the beauty of nature, the background to that wonderful night. On the other hand, this fusing of the nature-images with nature itself is perfect and complete only because Romeo and Juliet themselves have a personal relationship to the powers of night. A few lines from Juliet's monologue at the opening of the second scene of the third act may serve as example:

> Come, civil night,
> Thou sober-suited matron, all in black,
> And learn me how to lose a winning match,
> Play'd for a pair of stainless maidenhoods:
> Hood my unmann'd blood, bating in my cheeks,
> With thy black mantle; till strange love, grown bold,
> Think true love acted simple modesty.
> Come, night; come, Romeo; come, thou day in night;
> For thou wilt lie upon the wings of night
> Whiter than new snow on a raven's back.
> Come, gentle night, come, loving, black-brow'd night, . . .
>
> (iii. ii. 10)

Here the night is no longer something detached and extraneous, it appears as Juliet's ally, which she longs for and summons like a human being. The appeal to the night, recurring in this monologue four times, like the theme of a fugue, is intimately associated with the whole of Juliet's speech. The apostrophe of a personified element of nature is indeed a rhetorical artifice and a proven device, but how has convention once again been quickened with throbbing life and made to fit new aims! This great art of Shakespeare's of blending outer nature with the inner spirit of his characters, finds clear expression in the parting scene of the lovers (III. v.). Here the dawning day becomes to them a symbol of parting; but this interrelationship needs no artful constructions in expression, because the situation is so chosen that nature enters naturally and organically into the lovers' dialogue.

In *Romeo and Juliet* Shakespeare employed a special artifice by means of which the atmosphere of nature, though itself a symbol, is introduced in an organic manner. As Caroline Spurgeon was the first to show,[10] the two lovers appear to each other as light against a dark background, and all these light-images, in which sun, moon, the stars, lightning, heaven, day and night figure, thus aid in spreading over the whole play an intensive atmosphere of free nature. In the later tragedies we shall find in great perfection this art of characterization through images, whereby a particular atmosphere may be lent to the play.

That the "nature-imagery" grows so organically out of the self-expression of the characters is true in this play only of the speeches of Romeo and Juliet. The allusions which Benvolio and Montague make to Romeo's melancholy morning walks are still worded in the conventional manner:

> Madam, an hour before the worshipp'd sun
> Peer'd forth the golden window of the east,   (I. i. 125)

> But all so soon as the all-cheering sun,
> Should in the furthest east begin to draw
> The shady curtains from Aurora's bed,   (I. i. 139)

And when brother Lorenzo commences his monologue before his cell:

> The grey-eyed morn smiles on the frowning night,
> Chequering the eastern clouds with streaks of light,
> And flecked darkness like a drunkard reels
> From forth day's path and Titan's fiery wheels: (II. iii. 1)

[10] *Shakespeare's Imagery*, p. 310 sqq. Professor Spurgeon shows how the *light-image* pervades the whole play and how Shakespeare in his imagery continually represents the sudden flaming and vanishing of this tragic love as "brilliance swiftly quenched." [See this volume, pp. 61–65.]

This is still the old, somewhat declamatory method of introducing the scene with isolated nature-images.

Thus *Romeo and Juliet* shows at several points how Shakespeare produces a closer harmony between the imagery and the characters, between the inner and outer situation and the theme of the play. But even here, we have not yet what we should call "dramatic" imagery. With its rich poetic decoration, its abundance of epithets, its personifications, the imagery is still predominantly of a descriptive character. Thus the long description of Queen Mab appears as an extra-dramatic moment in the structure of the play. Less interrupting, but also exemplifying the tendency to elaborate, are the description of the effect which the poison will have upon Juliet (IV. i. 99) and the description of the apothecary and his dwelling by Romeo (V. i. 38, 69). In *Romeo and Juliet* Shakespeare is still writing in a style which leaves nothing unsaid. This tendency towards complete representation, clarification, amplification and description is nevertheless favourable to the development of a poetic diction of great wealth and colour in which the metaphorical element can freely unfold. For, compared to earlier plays, we find in *Romeo and Juliet* an increase of metaphors used where formerly a conceit or an elaborate comparison would have been inserted. These, it is true, have not yet disappeared, but the growing predilection for metaphors seems significant and suggests the way Shakespeare will go. Viewed from this angle, too, *Romeo and Juliet* appears as a play of transition.

How the Characters Talk

by James Sutherland

. . . In his novel, *Sandra Belloni,* George Meredith allows one of his characters to make a sweeping generalization about French writers. "Read their stereotyped descriptions," this character says. "They all say the same things. They have one big Gallic trumpet." [1] This sort of observation might get by at a London cocktail party, but would seem very flippant and ill-informed in a Parisian café: it is the gay and irresponsible remark of someone who is not really familiar with French literature. In the same way, many people are inclined to think of the blank verse of Shakespeare and his contemporaries as one big Elizabethan trumpet. We might conceivably say something like that of Marlowe's *Tamburlaine,* but we could not possibly speak of Shakespeare's continuously varied and responsive blank verse in such terms. Yet, just as we are no longer familiar with the eighteenth-century heroic couplet and are apt to find it monotonous where the contemporaries of Pope and Dr. Johnson would have found subtle variation, so we are no longer really familiar with blank verse as a dramatic medium, and are apt to miss all sorts of nuances and distinctions of tone and emphasis. The way in which Shakespeare's blank verse is often spoken by the modern actor makes me feel sure that I am not inventing or exaggerating this particular difficulty.

To make things as hard for myself as possible, I hope to show some of those differences of tone and intention and emphasis by examining a play which is usually thought of as being the very essence of Elizabethan poetic drama: *Romeo and Juliet.* "Read *Romeo and Juliet,*"

From "How the Characters Talk," by James Sutherland, in Shakespeare's World, *edited by James Sutherland and Joel Hurstfield (London: Edward Arnold (Publishers) Ltd., 1964), pp. 117–19, 122–28, 130–31. Copyright © 1964 by Edward Arnold (Publishers) Ltd. Reprinted by permission of the publisher. This selection omits discussion of speeches in other plays.*

[1] G. Meredith, *Sandra Belloni,* ch. viii.

Coleridge wrote, "—all is youth and spring; youth with all its follies, its virtues, its precipitancies; spring with its odours, its flowers, and its transiency; it is one and the same feeling that commences, goes through, and ends the play." He goes on to note that in Juliet "love has all that is tender and melancholy in the nightingale, all that is voluptuous in the rose, with whatever is sweet in the freshness of spring; but it ends with a long deep sigh like the last breeze of the Italian evening." [2] This is, of course, a good example of that impressionistic criticism which is at present so much out of fashion: one can well imagine the sort of punishment that would be meted out to any twentieth-century critic who wrote of *Romeo and Juliet* in such terms, always supposing that he could. Coleridge, at all events, concludes the passage with the statement that "This unity of feeling and character pervades every drama of Shakespeare." How true is that last sentence? And how true is it to say that "it is one and the same feeling that commences, goes through, and ends" *Romeo and Juliet*? I am not so foolish as to wish to suggest that this tragedy does not leave a unified impression on the mind; but the Shakespearian unity is one that comprehends and reconciles much diversity.

The play does not open, as Coleridge's words might lead us to expect, with young Romeo and Juliet alone in an Italian garden while the moon shines through the fruit trees and a nightingale sings with her breast against a thorn. It opens with two very ordinary examples of the common man, Sampson and Gregory, servants in the house of Capulet. They spend some time in what we would now call passing remarks, they make some poor puns, and soon, with that inevitability which we come to associate with the common man in Shakespeare, they are making mildly bawdy jokes. The nearest that their talk gets to love is that it turns on sex. But this is not the sort of love that Coleridge meant; it certainly hasn't "all that is tender and melancholy in the nightingale." After a few minutes of this cross-talk, "*Enter* ABRAHAM *and* BALTHASAR," and almost at once the swords are out and the four men are fighting. All this, of course, is highly relevant to the tragedy that Shakespeare is writing; it brings us face to face with the bitter quarrel that divides the Montagues from the Capulets. But it is very different from the sort of opening we should get in a Greek tragedy or in a neo-classical one.

At this point various gentlemen come in: Benvolio, followed immediately by Tybalt, then Capulet in his gown, and finally Montague. Because they are gentlemen they all speak in blank verse, and not in

[2] S. T. Coleridge, *Lectures and Notes on Shakespeare*, ed. T. Ashe, 1893, pp. 236–7.

the prose of their servants. It is the ordinary quarrelling speech of Shakespeare's upper-class characters; spirited, exclamatory, but none the less controlled and refined. While Lady Capulet and Lady Montague are striving to pacify them, the Prince enters with his attendants. He, too, speaks, of course, in blank verse. But does Shakespeare differentiate his speech from that of his subjects? I think we must say that he does, and I believe that the Elizabethan playgoer would have recognized the distinction at once.

> *Prince.* Rebellious subjects, enemies to peace,
> Profaners of this neighbour-stainéd steel—
> Will they not hear?—What ho! you men, you beasts,
> That quench the fire of your pernicious rage
> With purple fountains issuing from your veins,
> On pain of torture, from those bloody hands
> Throw your mistemper'd weapons to the ground,
> And hear the sentence of your moved prince . . .
>
>   (I. i. 87ff.)

It is, no doubt, only too easy to encourage ourselves to detect delicate gradations of style and tone where none exist, and to persuade ourselves, because we know that it is a prince who is talking to his subjects, that he is talking *like* a prince. But there is surely a special sort of grandiloquence in his manner of speaking; the voice of the ruler is clearly heard in such expressions as "profaners of this neighbour-stainéd steel" (with its impressive compound-adjective), in "the fire of your pernicious rage" quenched with "purple fountains" of blood, and in his demand that they throw their "mistemper'd weapons" to the ground. The diction is a little more artificial and polysyllabic than is normal. Shakespeare's kings and princes and dukes, too, are usually given a measured eloquence; they speak with a confident fullness of speech. I think we can detect this voice, the voice of authority, in Duke Theseus when he expresses his courteous willingness to listen to the rude play of the mechanicals (*Midsummer Night's Dream*, V. i), or in the various utterances of the banished duke in *As You Like It*.

                              *   *   *

. . . Having rebuked his rebellious subjects, the Prince leaves the stage, and the talk turns on Romeo. Lady Montague asks if anyone has seen him, and Benvolio answers her (I. i. 124ff.):

> Madam, an hour before the worshipp'd sun
> Peer'd forth the golden window of the east,
> A troubled mind drave me to walk abroad;

> Where, underneath the grove of sycamore
> That westward rooteth from the city's side,
> So early walking did I see your son. . . .

We have already met Benvolio and heard him talk, and this is not his normal voice. It is true that he is addressing a noble lady, and might be expected on that account to put on what used to be called company manners. But that isn't it. Her husband, old Montague, takes up the tale in exactly the same high-flown and artificial strain:

> Many a morning hath he there been seen,
> With tears augmenting the fresh morning's dew,
> Adding to clouds more clouds with his deep sighs;
> But all so soon as the all-cheering sun
> Should in the furthest east begin to draw
> The shady curtains from Aurora's bed,
> Away from light steals home my heavy son,
> And private in his chamber pens himself. . . .

The speeches we have been noticing so far have all been "in character," but these of Benvolio and Montague which I have just quoted must be accounted for on a different principle. While they do impart a certain amount of information about Romeo, they are primarily intended to make a direct emotional impression on the minds of the audience. The purpose of the highly-wrought language in these two speeches, with the sun peering forth from "the golden window of the east" and drawing "the shady curtains from Aurora's bed" is clearly to build up a romantic atmosphere for the first entrance of Romeo, who duly appears about a dozen lines later. The speeches of Benvolio and Montague, then, act in much the same way as dreamy incidental music to herald the entrance of the lovers. What is actually said is not negligible, but it is the way of saying it that really matters here; the connotation of the words is more important than their denotation. Shakespeare often wrote such speeches, more particularly in his earliest plays, to provide an emotional setting, to act as a sort of verbal limelight for a character or an approaching event.

* * *

. . . Romeo now enters. Romeo is in love, not yet with Juliet, but with Rosaline, who is cold to him. He speaks in quite a different way from Benvolio, who is with him, and from Mercutio a little later. The talk of Shakespeare's young men who are in love almost invariably runs into every kind of excess and hyperbole. "Now is he for the

numbers that Petrarch flowed in," says Mercutio as he sees the distracted Romeo coming towards him. In Shakespeare's world the young
men normally pursue the young women, and endeavour to win them
with a passionate eloquence. The young lover in Shakespeare therefore
behaves like the blackbird or thrush; he sits on the topmost branch
of the tree and sings to his mate. About the time that he wrote *Romeo
and Juliet* Shakespeare gave us this human bird-song in the series of
arias that he wrote for Valentine and Proteus in *The Two Gentlemen
of Verona,* and again in *Love's Labour's Lost,* where the king and his
three gentlemen all break into extravagant protestations of their love
for their respective ladies. Some years later Orlando in *As You Like It*
is still the typical Shakespearian lover. Romeo is entirely in the tradition:

> Why, then, O brawling love! O loving hate!
> O any thing! of nothing first create!
> O heavy lightness! serious vanity!
> Mis-shapen chaos of well-seeming forms!
> Feather of lead, bright smoke, cold fire, sick health!
> Still-waking sleep, that is not what it is! . . .   (I. i. 181ff.)

This is the Elizabethan lover, expressing himself in wild antitheses
which are a sort of verbal equivalent for his distracted state balanced
between two extremes ("feather of lead," "cold fire," etc.), and in conceits ("Love is a smoke raised by the fume of sighs") which serve
to represent the pleasing anguish of the lover, the grief of unrequited
love which is yet a happier condition than not loving at all would be.
Shakespeare may be writing in the Petrarchan convention on these
occasions, but he uses it quite seriously in tragedy, and he makes
good use of it in comedy when the intelligent young women who
are the objects of this extravagant adoration clamly prick the iridescent
bubbles which their lovers are blowing so beautifully.

This brings us to the end of the first scene, with Benvolio talking
good sense and Romeo still raving. But already, in this one scene,
we have had a considerable variety of speech because we have had a
corresponding variety of life—low life and high life, rebellion and
authority, romance and common sense.

The second scene, which opens with Capulet talking to Paris, offers
us at first nothing that we have not had before. But then Capulet
instructs one of his servants to deliver various invitations for the ball
he is giving that evening, and the servant is a chuckle-headed fellow,
who is, in fact, the equivalent of one of Shakespeare's blundering
clowns, and who speaks like one. In his brief muddled soliloquy he is

something quite different from the servants we met at the beginning of the play. Then we have Benvolio and Romeo again, much as before. This brings us to scene iii, and to the Nurse. The Nurse in *Romeo and Juliet* is one of Shakespeare's earliest triumphs in character study. Granville-Barker, who was not given to extravagant statements, and who as a producer of plays was exceptionally alive to the sort of distinctions that we are here considering, said of this famous character: "You may, indeed, take any sentence the Nurse speaks throughout the play, and only she could speak it." [3] The Nurse expresses herself both in verse and in prose; but when it is in verse it is of so familiar and conversational a kind that it tends to disappear as verse almost as completely as the verse does in Swift's poem, "The Humble Petition of Frances Harris." When we first meet her with Lady Capulet there is some discussion about how old Juliet is. The Nurse is sure she is not fourteen yet, and asks how long it is till Lammastide (I. iii. 15ff.):

> *Lady Cap.*   A fortnight and odd days.
> *Nurse.* Even or odd, of all days in the year,
>   Come Lammas-eve at night shall she be fourteen.
>   Susan and she—God rest all Christian souls!—
>   Were of an age: well, Susan is with God;
>   She was too good for me: but, as I said,
>   On Lammas-eve at night shall she be fourteen;
>   That shall she, marry; I remember it well.
>   'Tis since the earthquake now eleven years;
>   And she was wean'd—I never shall forget it—
>   Of all the days of the year, upon that day:
>   For I had then laid wormwood to my dug,
>   Sitting in the sun under the dove-house wall;
>   My lord and you were then at Mantua—
>   Nay, I do bear a brain—but, as I said,
>   When it did taste the wormwood on the nipple
>   Of my dug and felt it bitter, pretty fool,
>   To see it tetchy and fall out with the dug!
>   "Shake" quoth the dove-house: 'twas no need, I trow,
>   To bid me trudge:
>   And since that time it is eleven years;
>   For then she could stand alone; nay, by the rood,
>   She could have run and waddled all about;
>   For even the day before, she broke her brow:
>   And then my husband—God be with his soul!

[3] Harley Granville-Barker, *Prefaces to Shakespeare: Second Series*, 1944, p. 42.

'A was a merry man—took up the child:
"Yea," quoth he, "dost thou fall upon thy face?
Thou wilt fall backward when thou hast more wit;
Wilt thou not, Jule?" and, by my holidame,
The pretty wench left crying and said "Ay."
To see, now, how a jest shall come about!
I warrant, an I should live a thousand years,
I never should forget it. "Wilt thou not, Jule?" quoth he;
And, pretty fool, it stinted and said "Ay."

In trying to pin down what is characteristic in speech we have to take account of such considerations as the age, sex, social class and education of the speaker, and when we have allowed for all those there may not be much unaccounted for that we could attribute solely to the individual. The Nurse, for instance, has the garrulity of old age, and a tendency to slide into reminiscence. She recalls the earthquake, and that she was sitting in the sun under the dove-house wall when it happened, and that her master and mistress were away in Mantua at the time, and what her husband said when Juliet fell, and much else of the same purely factual kind. She has the animal vitality of healthy old age: once she is off on a reminiscence she is as irrepressible as the Wife of Bath, and has the same hearty vulgarity and confident femininity. Her lack of education is seen in the way that she joins her narrative together with a series of "Ands" and "Buts" and "Fors," the "Buts" and "Fors" being usually no more than simple connectives, and not really adversative or causal. She is endlessly repetitive, sometimes consciously so ("But, as I said"), more often unconsciously. (Her husband's brilliant joke, "Wilt thou not, Jule?" is repeated for the third time in her next speech.) She has the uneducated speaker's constant striving for emphasis, obtained characteristically by means of oaths ("marry," "by the rood"), by her wager, "I'll lay fourteen of my teeth," and by frequent exclamations ("God rest all Christian souls!," "pretty fool!," "God be with his soul!"). She keeps interrupting herself, breaking off as some irrelevant idea enters her head, i.e. some idea accidentally associated in time or place with what she is saying ("Well, Susan is with God," "For even a day before, she broke her brow"). Her whole speech, of course, is one vast irrelevance: the sole point at issue is the question: How old is Juliet? On this point, since I have quoted Coleridge at his most impressionistic, let me now quote him at his most psychological. "In all her recollections," Coleridge said of the Nurse, "she assists herself by the remembrance of visual circumstances. The great difference, in this respect, between the cultivated and the uncultivated mind

is this—that the cultivated mind will be found to recall the past by
certain regular trains of cause and effect; whereas, with the uncultivated mind, the past is recalled wholly by coincident images, or facts
which happened at the same time." [4] Linguistically, the words and
phrases the Nurse uses have often the marks of popular speech. I am
not sure about "dug." Although, as the O.E.D. tells us, the word "as
applied to a woman's breast [is] now contemptuous," it could have
been used quite inoffensively in the 1590s by Queen Elizabeth or the
Dark Lady of the Sonnets. But there is no question of the colloquial
nature of "That shall she, marry," " 'A was a merry man," or " 'twas no
need, I trow, to bid me trudge." To get the modern equivalent of
this last remark we should have to substitute something like "You
bet there was no need to tell *me* to hop it."

The Nurse, then, is a highly recognizable character. As such, she
brings us to the teasing question of how far Shakespeare was able to
individualize his characters by giving them a unique, or at least personal, mode of expression. Can we recognize, say, Falstaff, Cleopatra,
Antony, Richard II, Richard III, Shylock, Caliban, Hamlet, Hotspur,
Shallow, Coriolanus, Malvolio, Iago by the way they talk? Large claims
of this kind have been made by critics of many periods. Pope asserted
that "every single character in Shakespeare is as much an Individual
as those in Life itself; it is impossible to find any two alike." And he
went on to say: "Had all the Speeches been printed without the very
names of the Persons, I believe one might have apply'd them with
certainty to every speaker." [5] This is surely the language of exaggeration.
However well my students may know *Macbeth,* I hate to think what
they would do to me if I set them an essay in which I asked them to
contrast the characters of Lenox and Ross as they are revealed by their
speeches. Yet most of us probably feel that what Pope says of all Shakespeare's characters is at least true of many of them.

* * *

. . . In Act I, scene iv, we meet Mercutio, a young gentleman of
fashion, gay, mocking, *not* in love. His conversation, with a good deal
of *double entendre* and some polished phrases, anticipates in places
the talk of the libertine gallant of Restoration comedy. For Shakespeare he is almost unique, but Mercutio would have found many
young men like himself in the plays of Fletcher. The character in

[4] *Lectures and Notes on Shakespeare,* ed. cit., p. 87.
[5] *Eighteenth Century Essays on Shakespeare,* ed. D. Nichol Smith, 2nd ed., 1963,
p. 45.

Shakespeare who most resembles him is perhaps the irrepressible Lucio
in *Measure for Measure,* a young man quite distinct from Mercutio,
and yet in his free-spoken and irresponsible way talking very much
"according to the trick."

In scene v we have Capulet again, the very picture of fussy and
bustling old age, welcoming his guests with an old-world courtesy
and recalling the feats of his dancing youth. But Tybalt has caught
sight of Romeo, and complains to his uncle. The old man doesn't
want trouble at his party, and tries to pacify him. "I'll not endure
him," Tybalt says. Capulet now loses his temper (I. v. 8off.):

Cap.   He shall be endured:
    What, goodman boy! I say, he shall: go to;
    Am I the master here, or you? go to.
    You'll not endure him! God shall mend my soul!
    You'll make a mutiny among my guests!
    You will set cock-ahoop! You'll be the man!
Tyb. Why, uncle, 'tis a shame.
Cap.   Go to, go to;
    You are a saucy boy: is't so, indeed?
    This trick may chance to scathe you, I know what:
    You must contrary me! marry, 'tis time.—
    Well said, my hearts!—You are a princox; go:
    Be quiet, or—More light, more light!—For shame!
    I'll make you quiet.—What, cheerly, my hearts!

When I spoke earlier of Shakespeare's continuously varied and responsive blank verse it was this sort of passage that I had in mind.
The secret of it lies in a sort of contrapuntal effect between the formal
rhythm of the pentameter line and the rhythm of colloquial speech.
("He *shall be* endured" . . . "*You'll* not endure him" . . . "*You'll*
be the *man!*") In Capulet's second speech the effect is further heightened by his carrying on three conversations at once, with the mutinous
Tybalt, with his guests as they pass by, and with his servants. Shakespeare's ability to accommodate his verse to every movement of passion
grows more and more wonderful as his art matures.

Form and Formality in *Romeo and Juliet*

by Harry Levin

"Fain would I dwell on form—," says Juliet from her window to Romeo in the moonlit orchard below,

> Fain would I dwell on form—fain, fain deny
> What I have spoke; but farewell compliment! (II. ii. 88–89)[1]

Romeo has just violated convention, dramatic and otherwise, by overhearing what Juliet intended to be a soliloquy. Her cousin, Tybalt, had already committed a similar breach of social and theatrical decorum in the scene at the Capulets' feast, where he had also recognized Romeo's voice to be that of a Montague. There, when the lovers first met, the dialogue of their meeting had been formalized into a sonnet, acting out the conceit of his lips as pilgrims, her hand as a shrine, and his kiss as a culminating piece of stage-business, with an encore after an additional quatrain: "You kiss by th' book" (I. v. 112). Neither had known the identity of the other; and each, upon finding it out, responded with an ominous exclamation coupling love and death (120, 140). The formality of their encounter was framed by the ceremonious character of the scene, with its dancers, its masquers, and—except for Tybalt's stifled outburst—its air of old-fashioned hospitality. "We'll measure them a measure," Benvolio had proposed; but Romeo, unwilling to join the dance, had resolved to be an onlooker and carry a torch (I. iv. 10). That torch may have burned symbolically, but not for Juliet; indeed, as we are inclined to forget with Romeo, he attended the feast in order to see the dazzling but soon eclipsed Rosaline. Rosaline's prior effect upon him is all that we ever learn about her; yet it has been enough to make Romeo, when he was presented to us, a

"Form and Formality in Romeo and Juliet*" by Harry Levin. From* Shakespeare Quarterly, *XI (1960), 3–11. Reprinted by permission of the author and The Shakespeare Association of America, Inc.*

[1] Line-references are to the separate edition of G. L. Kittredge's text (Boston, 1940).

virtual stereotype of the romantic lover. As such, he has protested a
good deal too much in his preliminary speeches, utilizing the conventional phrases and standardized images of Elizabethan eroticism, bandy-
ing generalizations, paradoxes, and sestets with Benvolio, and taking a
quasi-religious vow which his introduction to Juliet would ironically
break (I. ii. 92–97). Afterward this role has been reduced to absurdity
by the humorous man, Mercutio, in a mock-conjuration evoking Venus
and Cupid and the inevitable jingle of "love" and "dove" (II. i. 10).
The scene that follows is actually a continuation, marked in neither
the Folios nor the Quartos, and linked with what has gone before by
a somewhat eroded rhyme.

> 'Tis in vain
> To seek him here that means not to be found,

Benvolio concludes in the absence of Romeo (41, 42). Whereupon the
latter, on the other side of the wall, chimes in:

> He jests at scars that never felt a wound.   (II. ii. 1)

Thus we stay behind, with Romeo, when the masquers depart. Juliet,
appearing at the window, does not hear his descriptive invocation. Her
first utterance is the very sigh that Mercutio burlesqued in the fore-
going scene: "Ay, me!" (II. ii. 25). Then, believing herself to be alone
and masked by the darkness, she speaks her mind in sincerity and simplicity. She calls into question not merely Romeo's name but—by
implication—all names, forms, conventions, sophistications, and arbitrary dictates of society, as opposed to the appeal of instinct directly
conveyed in the odor of a rose. When Romeo takes her at her word
and answers, she is startled and even alarmed for his sake; but she does
not revert to courtly language.

> I would not for the world they saw thee here,

she tells him, and her monosyllabic directness inspires the matching
cadence of his response:

> And but thou love me, let them find me here. (77, 79)

She pays incidental tribute to the proprieties with her passing suggestion that, had he not overheard her, she would have dwelt on form,
pretended to be more distant, and played the not impossible part of
the captious beloved. But farewell compliment! Romeo's love for Juliet
will have an immediacy which cuts straight through the verbal em-
bellishment that has obscured his infatuation with Rosaline. That
shadowy creature, having served her Dulcinea-like purpose, may well

be forgotten. On the other hand, Romeo has his more tangible foil in the person of the County Paris, who is cast in that ungrateful part which the Italians call *terzo incòmodo,* the inconvenient third party, the unwelcome member of an amorous triangle. As the official suitor of Juliet, his speeches are always formal, and often sound stilted or priggish by contrast with Romeo's. Long after Romeo has abandoned his sonneteering, Paris will pronounce a sestet at Juliet's tomb (V. iii. 11–16). During their only colloquy, which occurs in Friar Laurence's cell, Juliet takes on the sophisticated tone of Paris, denying his claims and disclaiming his compliments in brisk stichomythy. As soon as he leaves, she turns to the Friar, and again—as so often in intimate moments—her lines fall into monosyllables:

> O, shut the door! and when thou hast done so,
> Come weep with me—past hope, past cure, past help! (IV. i. 44–45)

Since the suit of Paris is the main subject of her conversations with her parents, she can hardly be sincere with them. Even before she met Romeo, her consent was hedged in prim phraseology:

> I'll look to like, if looking liking move.   (I. iii. 97)

And after her involvement she becomes adept in the stratagems of mental reservation, giving her mother equivocal rejoinders and rousing her father's anger by chopping logic (III. v. 69–205). Despite the intervention of the Nurse on her behalf, her one straightforward plea is disregarded. Significantly Lady Capulet, broaching the theme of Paris in stiffly appropriate couplets, has compared his face to a volume:[2]

> This precious book of love, this unbound lover,
> To beautify him only lacks a cover.
> The fish lives in the sea, and 'tis much pride
> The fair without the fair within to hide.   (I. iii. 89–90)

That bookish comparison, by emphasizing the letter at the expense of the spirit, helps to lend Paris an aspect of unreality; to the Nurse, more ingenuously, he is "a man of wax" (76). Later Juliet will echo Lady Capulet's metaphor, transferring it from Paris to Romeo:

> Was ever book containing such vile matter
> So fairly bound?   (III. ii. 83–84)

Here, on having learned that Romeo has just slain Tybalt, she is

---

[2] On the long and rich history of this trope, see the sixteenth chapter of E. R. Curtius, *European Literature and the Latin Middle Ages,* tr. W. R. Trask (New York, 1953).

undergoing a crisis of doubt, a typically Shakespearian recognition of the difference between appearance and reality. The fair without may not cover a fair within, after all. Her unjustified accusations, leading up to her rhetorical question, form a sequence of oxymoronic epithets: "Beautiful tyrant, fiend angelical, . . . honorable villain!" (75–79) W. H. Auden, in a recent comment on these lines,[3] cannot believe they would come from a heroine who had been exclaiming shortly before: "Gallop apace, you fiery-footed steeds . . . !" Yet Shakespeare has been perfectly consistent in suiting changes of style to changes of mood. When Juliet feels at one with Romeo, her intonations are genuine; when she feels at odds with him, they should be unconvincing. The attraction of love is played off against the revulsion from books, and coupled with the closely related themes of youth and haste, in one of Romeo's long-drawn-out leavetakings:

> Love goes toward love as schoolboys from their books;
> But love from love, towards school with heavy looks.   (II. ii. 157–158)

The school for these young lovers will be tragic experience. When Romeo, assuming that Juliet is dead and contemplating his own death, recognizes the corpse of Paris, he will extend the image to cover them both:

> O give me thy hand,
> One writ with me in sour misfortune's book!   (V. iii. 82)

It was this recoil from bookishness, together with the farewell to compliment, that animated *Love's Labour's Lost,* where literary artifice was so ingeniously deployed against itself, and Berowne was taught— by an actual heroine named Rosaline—that the best books were women's eyes. Some of Shakespeare's other early comedies came even closer to adumbrating certain features of *Romeo and Juliet*: notably, *The Two Gentlemen of Verona,* with its locale, its window scene, its friar and rope, its betrothal and banishment, its emphasis upon the vagaries of love. Shakespeare's sonnets and erotic poems had won for him the reputation of an English Ovid. *Romeo and Juliet,* the most elaborate product of his so-called lyrical period, was his first successful experiment in tragedy.[4] Because of that very success, it is hard for us to

---

[3] In the paper-bound Laurel Shakespeare, ed. Francis Fergusson (New York, 1958), p. 26.

[4] H. B. Charlton, in his British Academy lecture for 1939, *"Romeo and Juliet" as an Experimental Tragedy,* has considered the experiment in the light of Renaissance critical theory [see this volume, pp. 49–60 for Charlton's adaptation of this lecture].

realize the full extent of its novelty, though scholarship has lately been reminding us of how it must have struck contemporaries.[5] They would have been surprised, and possibly shocked, at seeing lovers taken so seriously. Legend, it had been heretofore taken for granted, was the proper matter for serious drama; romance was the stuff of the comic stage. Romantic tragedy—*"an excellent conceited Tragedie of Romeo and Juliet,"* to cite the title-page of the First Quarto—was one of those contradictions in terms which Shakespeare seems to have delighted in resolving. His innovation might be described as transcending the usages of romantic comedy, which are therefore very much in evidence, particularly at the beginning. Subsequently, the leading characters acquire together a deeper dimension of feeling by expressly repudiating the artificial language they have talked and the superficial code they have lived by. Their formula might be that of the anti-Petrarchan sonnet:

Foole said My muse to mee, looke in thy heart and write.[6]

An index of this development is the incidence of rhyme, heavily concentrated in the First Act, and its gradual replacement by a blank verse which is realistic or didactic with other speakers and unprecedentedly limpid and passionate with the lovers. "Love has no need of euphony," the eminent Russian translator of the play, Boris Pasternak, has commented. "Truth, not sound, dwells in its heart." [7]

Comedy set the pattern of courtship, as formally embodied in a dance. The other *genre* of Shakespeare's earlier stagecraft, history, set the pattern of conflict, as formally embodied in a duel. *Romeo and Juliet* might also be characterized as an anti-revenge play, in which hostile emotions are finally pacified by the interplay of kindlier ones. Romeo sums it up in his prophetic oxymorons:

Here's much to do with hate, but more with love.
Why then, O brawling love! O loving hate!
O anything, of nothing first create!   (I. i. 162–164)

And Paris, true to type, waxes grandiose in lamenting Juliet:

O love! O life! not life, but love in death!   (IV. v. 58)

---

[5] Especially F. M. Dickey, *Not Wisely But Too Well: Shakespeare's Love Tragedies* (San Marino, 1957), pp. 63–88 [see this volume, pp. 99–100].

[6] Sir Philip Sidney, *Astrophel and Stella,* ed. Albert Feuillerat (Cambridge, 1922), p. 243.

[7] Boris Pasternak, "Translating Shakespeare," tr. Manya Harari, *The Twentieth Century,* CLXIV, 979 (September, 1958), p. 217.

Here, if we catch the echo from Hieronimo's lament in *The Spanish Tragedy,*

> O life! no life, but lively form of death,

we may well note that the use of antithesis, which is purely decorative with Kyd, is functional with Shakespeare. The contrarieties of his plot are reinforced on the plane of imagery by omnipresent reminders of light and darkness,[8] youth and age, and many other antitheses subsumed by the all-embracing one of Eros and Thanatos, the *leitmotif* of the *Liebestod,* the myth of the tryst in the tomb. This attraction of ultimate opposites—which is succinctly implicit in the Elizabethan ambiguity of the verb *to die*—is generalized when the Friar rhymes "womb" with "tomb," and particularized when Romeo hails the latter place as "thou womb of death" (I. iii. 9, 10; V. iii. 45). Hence the "extremities" of the situation, as the Prologue to the Second Act announces, are tempered "with extreme sweet" (14). Those extremes begin to meet as soon as the initial prologue, in a sonnet disarmingly smooth, has set forth the feud between the two households, "Where civil blood makes civil hands unclean" (4). Elegant verse yields to vulgar prose, and to an immediate riot, as the servants precipitate a renewal—for the third time—of their masters' quarrel. The brawl of Act I is renewed again in the *contretemps* of Act III and completed by the swordplay of Act V. Between the street-scenes, with their clashing welter of citizens and officers, we shuttle through a series of interiors, in a flurry of domestic arrangements and family relationships. The house of the Capulets is the logical center of action, and Juliet's chamber its central sanctum. Consequently, the sphere of privacy encloses Acts II and IV, in contradistinction to the public issues raised by the alternating episodes. The temporal alternation of the play, in its accelerating continuity, is aptly recapitulated by the impatient rhythm of Capulet's speech:

> Day, night, late, early,
> At home, abroad, alone, in company,
> Waking or sleeping . . .   (III. v. 177–179)

The alignment of the *dramatis personae* is as symmetrical as the antagonism they personify. It is not without relevance that the names of the feuding families, like the Christian names of the hero and heroine, are metrically interchangeable (though "Juliet" is more frequently a

[8] Caroline Spurgeon, *Shakespeare's Imagery and What It Tells Us* (New York, 1936), pp. 310–316 [see this volume, pp. 61–65].

trochee than an amphimacer). Tybalt the Capulet is pitted against Benvolio the Montague in the first street-fight, which brings out—with parallel stage-directions—the heads of both houses restrained by respective wives. Both the hero and heroine are paired with others, Rosaline and Paris, and admonished by elderly confidants, the Friar and the Nurse. Escalus, as Prince of Verona, occupies a superior and neutral position; yet, in the interchange of blood for blood, he loses "a brace of kinsman," Paris and Mercutio (V. iii. 295). Three times he must quell and sentence the rioters before he can pronounce the final sestet, restoring order to the city-state through the lovers' sacrifice. He effects the resolution by summoning the patriarchal enemies, from their opposite sides, to be reconciled. "Capulet, Montague," he sternly arraigns them, and the polysyllables are brought home by monosyllabics:

> See what a scourge is laid upon your hate
> That heaven finds means to kill your joys with love.   (291–293)

The two-sided counterpoise of the dramatic structure is well matched by the dynamic symmetry of the antithetical style. One of its peculiarities, which surprisingly seems to have escaped the attention of commentators, is a habit of stressing a word by repeating it within a line, a figure which may be classified in rhetoric as a kind of *ploce*. I have cited a few examples incidentally; let me now underline the device by pointing out a few more. Thus Montague and Capulet are accused of forcing their parties

> To wield old partisans in hands as old,
> Cank'red with peace, to part your cank'red hate.   (I. i. 100, 102)

This double instance, along with the wordplay on "cank'red," suggests the embattled atmosphere of partisanship through the halberds; and it is further emphasized in Benvolio's account of the fray:

> Came more and more, and fought on part and part.   (122)

The key-words are not only doubled but affectionately intertwined, when Romeo confides to the Friar:

> As mine on hers, so hers is set on mine.   (II. iii. 59)

Again, he conveys the idea of reciprocity by declaring that Juliet returns "grace for grace and love for love" (86). The Friar's warning hints at poetic justice:

> These violent delights have violent ends.   (II. vi. 9)

Similarly Mercutio, challenged by Tybalt, turns "point to point," and the Nurse finds Juliet—in *antimetabole*—"Blubb'ring and weeping, weeping and blubbering" (III. ii. 165; iii. 87). Statistics would prove illusory, because some repetitions are simply idiomatic, grammatical, or—in the case of old Capulet or the Nurse—colloquial. But it is significant that the play contains well over a hundred such lines, the largest number being in the First Act and scarcely any left over for the Fifth.

The significance of this tendency toward reduplication, both stylistic and structural, can perhaps be best understood in the light of Bergson's well-known theory of the comic: the imposition of geometrical form upon the living data of formless consciousness. The stylization of love, the constant pairing and counter-balancing, the *quid pro quo* of Capulet and Montague, seem mechanical and unnatural. Nature has other proponents besides the lovers, especially Mercutio their fellow victim, who bequeathes his curse to both their houses. His is likewise an ironic end, since he has been as much a satirist of "the new form" and Tybalt's punctilio in duelling "by the book of arithmetic" as of "the numbers that Petrarch flowed in" and Romeo's affectations of gallantry (II. iv. 34, 38; III. i. 104). Mercutio's interpretation of dreams, running counter to Romeo's premonitions, is naturalistic, not to say Freudian; Queen Mab operates through fantasies of wish-fulfilment, bringing love to lovers, fees to lawyers, and tithe-pigs to parsons; the moral is that desires can be mischievous. In his repartee with Romeo, Mercutio looks forward to their fencing with Tybalt; furthermore he charges the air with bawdy suggestions that—in spite of the limitations of Shakespeare's theatre, its lack of actresses and absence of close-ups— love may have something to do with sex, if not with lust, with the physical complementarity of male and female.[9] He is abetted, in that respect, by the malapropistic garrulity of the Nurse, Angelica, who is naturally bound to Juliet through having been her wet-nurse, and who has lost the infant daughter that might have been Juliet's age. None the less, her crotchety hesitations are contrasted with Juliet's youthful ardors when the Nurse acts as go-between for Romeo. His counsellor, Friar Laurence, makes a measured entrance with his sententious couplets on the uses and abuses of natural properties, the medicinal and poisonous effects of plants:

> For this, being smelt, with that part cheers each part;
> Being tasted, slays all senses with the heart.   (II. iii. 25, 26)

[9] Coleridge's persistent defense of Shakespeare against the charge of gross language does more credit to that critic's high-mindedness than to his discernment. The concentrated ribaldry of the gallants in the street (II. iv) is deliberately contrasted with the previous exchange between the lovers in the orchard.

His watchword is "Wisely and slow," yet he contributes to the grief at the sepulcher by ignoring his own advice, "They stumble that run fast" (94).[10] When Romeo upbraids him monosyllabically,

> Thou canst not speak of that thou doest not feel,

it is the age-old dilemma that separates the generations: *Si jeunesse savait, si vieillesse pouvait* (III. iii. 64). Banished to Mantua, Romeo has illicit recourse to the Apothecary, whose shop—envisaged with Flemish precision—unhappily replaces the Friar's cell, and whose poison is the sinister counterpart of Laurence's potion.

Against this insistence upon polarity, at every level, the mutuality of the lovers stands out, the one organic relation amid an overplus of stylized expressions and attitudes. The naturalness of their diction is artfully gained, as we have noticed, through a running critique of artificiality. In drawing a curtain over the consummation of their love, Shakespeare heralds it with a prothalamium and follows it with an epithalamium. Juliet's "Gallop apace, you fiery-footed steeds," reversing the Ovidian *"lente currite, noctis equi,"* is spoken "alone" but in breathless anticipation of a companion (III. ii. 1). After having besought the day to end, the sequel to her solo is the duet in which she begs the night to continue. In the ensuing *débat* of the nightingale and the lark, a refinement upon the antiphonal song of the owl and the cuckoo in *Love's Labour's Lost,* Romeo more realistically discerns "the herald of the morn" (III. v. 6). When Juliet reluctantly agrees, "More light and light it grows," he completes the paradox with a doubly reduplicating line:

> More light and light—more dark and dark our woes!   (35, 36)

The precariousness of their union, formulated arithmetically by the Friar as "two in one" (II. vi. 37), is brought out by the terrible loneliness of Juliet's monologue upon taking the potion:

> My dismal scene I needs must act alone.   (IV. iii. 19)

Her utter singleness, as an only child, is stressed by her father and mourned by her mother:

> But one, poor one, one poor and loving child.   (v. 46)

Tragedy tends to isolate where comedy brings together, to reveal the uniqueness of individuals rather than what they have in common with

---

[10] This is the leading theme of the play, in the interpretation of Brents Stirling, *Unity in Shakespearian Tragedy: The Interplay of Themes and Characters* (New York, 1956), pp. 10–25.

others. Asking for Romeo's profession of love, Juliet anticipates: "I
know thou wilt say 'Ay' " (II. ii. 90). That monosyllable of glad assent
was the first she ever spoke, as we know from the Nurse's childish
anecdote (I. iii. 48). Later, asking the Nurse whether Romeo has been
killed, Juliet pauses self-consciously over the pun between "Ay" and
"I" or "eye":

> Say thou but "I,"
> And that bare vowel "I" shall poison more
> Than the death-darting eye of cockatrice.
> I am not I, if there be such an "I";
> Or those eyes shut that make thee answer "I."
> If he be slain, say "I"; or if not, "no."
> Brief sounds determine of my weal or woe.   (III. ii. 45-51)

Her identification with him is negated by death, conceived as a shut or
poisoning "eye," which throws the pair back upon their single selves.
Each of them dies alone—or, at all events, in the belief that the other
lies dead, and without the benefit of a recognition-scene. Juliet, of
course, is still alive; but she has already voiced her death-speech in the
potion scene. With the dagger, her last words, though richly symbolic,
are brief and monosyllabic:

> This is thy sheath; there rest, and let me die.   (V. iii. 170)

The sense of vicissitude is re-enacted through various gestures of
staging; Romeo and Juliet experience their exaltation "aloft" on the
upper stage; his descent via the rope is, as she fears, toward the tomb
(III. v. 56).[11] The antonymous adverbs *up* and *down* figure, with increasing prominence, among the brief sounds that determine Juliet's
woe (e.g., V. ii. 209-210). The overriding pattern through which she
and Romeo have been trying to break—call it Fortune, the stars, or
what you will—ends by closing in and breaking them; their private
world disappears, and we are left in the social ambiance again. Capulet's house has been bustling with preparations for a wedding, the
happy ending of comedy. The news of Juliet's death is not yet tragic
because it is premature; but it introduces a peripety which will become
the starting point for *Hamlet*.

> All things that we ordained festival
> Turn from their office to black funeral—

---

[11] One of the more recent and pertinent discussions of staging is that of Richard
Hosley, "The Use of the Upper Stage in *Romeo and Juliet*," *Shakespeare Quarterly*,
V, [no.] 4 (Autumn, 1954), 371-379.

the old man cries, and his litany of contraries is not less poignant because he has been so fond of playing the genial host:

> Our instruments to melancholy bells,
> Our wedding cheer to a sad burial feast;
> Our solemn hymns to sullen dirges change;
> Our bridal flowers serve for a buried corse;
> And all things change them to the contrary.   (IV. v. 84–90)

His lamentation, in which he is joined by his wife, the Nurse, and Paris, reasserts the formalities by means of what is virtually an operatic quartet. Thereupon the music becomes explicit, when they leave the stage to the Musicians, who have walked on with the County Paris. Normally these three might play during the *entr'acte,* but Shakespeare has woven them into the dialogue terminating the Fourth Act.[12] Though their art has the power of soothing the passions and thereby redressing grief, as the comic servant Peter reminds them with a quotation from Richard Edward's lyric *In Commendacion of Musicke,* he persists in his query: "Why 'silver sound'?" (131) Their answers are those of mere hirelings, who can indifferently change their tune from a merry dump to a doleful one, so long as they are paid with coin of the realm. Yet Peter's riddle touches a deeper chord of correspondence, the interconnection between discord and harmony, between impulse and discipline. "Consort," which can denote a concert or a companionship, can become the fighting word that motivates the unharmonious pricksong of the duellists (III. i. 48). The "sweet division" of the lark sounds harsh and out of tune to Juliet, since it proclaims that the lovers must be divided (v. 29). Why "silver sound"? Because Romeo, in the orchard, has sworn by the moon

> That tips with silver all these fruit-tree tops.   (II. i. 108)

Because Shakespeare, transposing sights and sounds into words, has made us imagine

> How silver-sweet sound lovers' tongues by night,
> Like softest music to attending ears!   (167–168)

Harvard University

[12] Professor F. T. Bowers reminds me that inter-act music was probably not a regular feature of public performance when *Romeo and Juliet* was first performed. Some early evidence for it has been gathered by T. S. Graves in "The Act-Time in Elizabethan Theatres," *Studies in Philology,* XII, [no.] 3 (July, 1915), 120–124—notably contemporary sound cues, written into a copy of the Second Quarto and cited by Malone. But if—as seems likely—such practices were exceptional, then Shakespeare was innovating all the farther.

PART TWO

View Points

J. Dover Wilson

Let him speak through the play which above all others belongs to
the young, his *Romeo and Juliet*. Written at the height of his Elizabethan gaiety, this tragic tale of star-crossed lovers is shot with comic
colour and rich in comic characters, among whom Mercutio and the
Nurse stand out pre-eminent. By what right have these reprobates
thrust themselves into so tender, so sublime a drama of young love?
The answer is that they are the two pillars which support the whole
dramatic structure. For the lovers, in the great scenes where they are
together, scenes more like opera than drama, chant their passion to
each other in immortal verse but tell us little about themselves. Yet
somehow Shakespeare must convince us of their reality, must assure us
that they are creatures of flesh and blood. He does so by placing characters of the utmost vivacity at their side—the Nurse beside Juliet and
Mercutio beside Romeo. Furthermore, both Mercutio and the Nurse
are coarse and harp upon the physical basis of love. He is full of the
bawdy talk that hot-blooded young men affect; and she prattles after
the manner of old peasant women. Is not Shakespeare stooping to tickle
the palate of "those wretched beings" his audience? Are not such passages just "sallets to make the matter savoury," outrageous excrescences
upon the greatest of modern love-poems? On the contrary, they are as
essential to the tone of the play as the characters which speak them
are to the play's structure. Once again the magician is assuring us of
reality. He is proving that the marvellous blossom of love which forms
the main theme of the story is not a mere poet's dream, a pleasing
fancy, but a piece of real life rooted deep in the crude common soil of
human nature, the nature we all know so well, too well. He is persuad-
ing young readers or spectators, boys and girls of all types, that the
passion of Mercutio's bosom friend for a mistress suckled at the Nurse's

From "The Elizabethan Shakespeare" by J. Dover Wilson, in Proceedings of the
British Academy, *XV (London: Oxford University Press, 1929), 123–24. Reprinted
by permission of the publisher.*

breast is a passion possible for themselves; and by making such splendour seem possible he is adding meaning and sanctification to their own little loves. It is just because Shakespeare conceals nothing and condemns nothing—because he is so utterly unlike a school-master or a preacher or a professor—that the young feel safe with him. And having gained their confidence he may lead them where he will, to endure the purging fires of *Macbeth* and *Othello,* to share the crucifixion and redemption of Lear, to win through to the haven of atonement and forgiveness in the enchanted island.

Franklin M. Dickey

. . . In the course of love comedy there is much laughter at love and sex, much ingenious and burlesque rhetoric for the amusement of the audience and the cooler characters of the play. The love play usually contains one or more commentators who underline the folly of love, even if they themselves become subject to its tyranny. *Romeo and Juliet* conforms surprisingly to this formula.

The melancholy lover whose humors had amused English audiences for the better part of a century is represented in Romeo; the commentator who extracts all the sport he can from the lover's folly is Mercutio. There is no witty Mercutio in Brooke; in Shakespeare he serves not only as Tybalt's victim but also to complete the comic *dramatis personae* of the love play. Like Speed in *Two Gentlemen* or the Vice, described in the title of Heywood's play as "nother lover nor beloved," Mercutio "jests at scars that never felt a wound." But like his predecessors he does more than supply comic contrast with the lover whose wounds are real. Mercutio serves to keep us from taking the lovers too seriously at the beginning of the play, and contributes to the richness of the lyrical comedy of the balcony scene.

The supposition that Shakespeare modeled his love tragedy on patterns of comedy, the usual vehicle for love, is strengthened when we look at the remaining comic characters in the first two acts. In spite of the gloomy Prologue, the tone at the opening curtain is extravagantly comic, so that when young love enters it is in key with the lively humor of the rest of the cast. Whatever his "influences," Shakespeare has employed the methods of Italian or Roman comedy in his characterization of the servants, the antics of Capulet and Montague,

From **Not Wisely But Too Well: Shakespeare's Love Tragedies** by *Franklin M. Dickey* (*San Marino, Calif.: The Huntington Library, 1957*), *pp. 72–75. Copyright 1957 by Henry E. Huntington Library & Art Gallery. Reprinted by permission of the publisher.*

and the garrulity of Juliet's Nurse, who corresponds to the bawd of classical comedy. All are familiar types, and their intrusion upon Brooke's straight-faced plot is in keeping with the usual treatment of love on the English stage.

Indeed our first sight of the "ancient grudge" which must end with "the misadventur'd piteous overthrows" of the lovers contains almost more horseplay than swordplay. The story as Shakespeare found it in Brooke contains no hint of this burlesque but preserves the decorum of a tragic poem. Brooke's feud must be taken seriously, and his two fathers are not in the least amusing. Although Shakespeare inserts reminders that hatred will produce tragedy, the tone and manner of his early presentation of this passion is alien to Brooke's tragic formula.

The tone and manner of the opening are not, however, alien to the treatment of testy old fathers in Italian and in Roman comedy. Winifred Smith has printed her translation of one of Scala's *scenari*, *Li Tragici Successi*, under the title "A Comic Version of Romeo and Juliet." [1] In this typical improvised tragicomedy the heads of the two quarreling houses are a Pantalone and a Gratiano, the stock irate fathers of the Italian stage. From the sketchy scenario it is impossible to tell except by inference what the old men said or did; we may assume though that they acted like all the other old men of the highly conventional *commedia dell' arte*, and that their impotent rage made the audience laugh.

If there is nothing to prove that Shakespeare knew this play, there is little doubt that by the time he wrote *Romeo and Juliet* he was familiar both with the stereotypes of improvised comedy and the stock figures of Plautus.[2] Among the constant plot elements in these plays were the pair of young lovers and their elderly grotesque fathers or guardians whose crotchets stood in the way of love. It seems clear that Shakespeare's old fathers, who owe nothing to Brooke for their high jinks, derive from these comic types and that the whole conception of the opening feud is similar to that of Latin comedy and its successor, the *commedia dell' arte*.

Finally we realize how much Shakespeare is indebted to comic traditions when we look at the Nurse. She inherits the nature of the bawd of Roman comedy and the *ruffiana* of the *commedia dell' arte*. Like these she is lewd and talkative and full of advice, largely mistaken, on affairs of the heart. Too old for marriage herself, she looks back

---

[1] *MP* [*Modern Philology*], VII (1909), pp. 217–220.

[2] See O. J. Campbell, *"Two Gentlemen of Verona* [an Italian Comedy," *Studies in Shakespeare, Milton and Donne* (New York, 1925)]. See also George E. Duckworth, *The Nature of Roman Comedy* (Princeton, 1952), pp. 412–418.

to the pleasures of her youth, sighs for her dead husband even as she curses mankind, and gets vicarious pleasure from the contemplation of Juliet's wedded nights. All that love means to her is "happy nights to happy days." Mercutio suggests her classical heritage when he shouts at her approach, "A bawd, a bawd, a bawd! So ho!" (II, iv, 136). Her method of delivering news is that of the "running slaves" of Plautus.[3] It is also one of the *lazzi* of the servants in the *commedia dell' arte*.[4] When Juliet sends her out to meet Romeo the old woman takes an unconscionably long time about her errand and when she returns to her mistress, gasps and pants, complaining about her old bones and shortness of breath until Juliet is frantic. At last after a long harangue full of irrelevancies, she reveals her tremendously important message in an offhand manner.

In Scene ii of Act II again we have the same device; the Nurse hobbles in with the dreadful tidings of Tybalt's death, but is so long-winded in giving the substance of her news that Juliet believes Romeo killed. In this same scene, after Juliet has finally learned that Tybalt is dead and Romeo banished, the Nurse casually reveals the news she should have given at the first, that Romeo is safely hidden in Friar Laurence's cell and waits for word from his love. All these incidents are Shakespeare's invention. Brooke's Nurse is loquacious but no more; she neither talks bawdily nor delays in giving her news.

In the end when she advises Juliet to go ahead and marry Paris since Romeo will be out of the way, Juliet's epithet "ancient damnation" condemns her like the Vice of comedy to a just oblivion. Her patent sexuality serves to set off Juliet's tender and legitimate rapture. It also serves as an antidote to the romantic conception of love. We enjoy old Angelica and Shakespeare meant us to; we laugh not only at her but with her. Her presence reminds us continually that even the most exalted passion of the lovers contains a tincture of sexuality, and that sexuality may be a laughable human frailty.

Winifred Nowottny

Brought to the bar of criticism, the play will seem short of tragic only if we prescribe what a tragedy must be; for instance, that it must

---

From "*Shakespeare's Tragedies*," by *Winifred Nowottny, in* Shakespeare's World, edited by James Sutherland and Joel Hurstfield (London: Edward Arnold (Publishers) Ltd., 1964), pp. 49–51, 53. Copyright © 1964 by Edward Arnold (Publishers) Ltd. Reprinted by permission of the publisher.

[3] See Duckworth, *The Complete Roman Drama* (New York, 1942), I, xxvii.
[4] See K. M. Lea, *Italian Popular Comedy* (Oxford, 1934), I, 69.

be about moral choice. As to its language, this will seem extravagant only if we demand that Romeo and Juliet should be less extravagant in feeling than they are, and that they should talk language such as men and women do use when they are not in love and not living in the sixteenth century. For, as Ringler points out, in his commentary on a sonnet in Sidney's *Astrophel and Stella,* "The Elizabethans regularly indicate heightened emotion by exaggerated elaboration of conceit." [1] Sidney, in order to express Stella's complete ascendency over him, uses this highly artificial conceit:

> When sorrow (using mine owne fier's might)
> Melts downe his lead into my boyling brest,
> Through that darke fornace to my hart opprest,
> There shines a joy from thee my only light;
>
> .   .   .   .   #
>
> So strangely (alas) thy works in me prevaile,
>   That in my woes for thee thou art my joy,
>   And in my joyes for thee my only annoy.

The style of *Romeo and Juliet* is not more fanciful or artificial than this.

It might be objected that an elaborate style will do for a sonneteer but not for a dramatist. There is, however, very good reason why Romeo the lover, and Juliet, too, should talk like a sonneteer. The play was written in the heyday of the sonnet, and the language of the sonnet was the language of love. The kind of love Petrarch had celebrated was often regarded as an experience which lifted a man above himself, as an exaltation of the spirit so spectacular that only religious experience could compete with it for intensity. It would hardly have been possible for Shakespeare, writing about idealistic passion at a time when the sonnet vogue was at its height, to ignore the sonneteers' language for it.

And, indeed, the convention was very useful for his purposes. The fact that it was, at this time, so highly developed, made it possible for him to present the experience of his hero and heroine in language which could claim to be universal; it is the language of lovers in general, not of Romeo and Juliet in particular; they do not need individual characters in order to be able to speak as they do. None the less, they are sufficiently individualized, within the world of the play

[1] William A. Ringler, jun. (ed.), *The Poems of Sir Philip Sidney* (Oxford, 1962), p. 491.

itself, by the fact that to be in their state of mind is to be in a world of
one's own. Their world, to Mercutio, is absurd; it is a closed world
to the Nurse; it is a world Capulet has no time for, and one of whose
wilfulness the Friar disapproves. This contrast between the world of
lovers and the world of other people is itself a universal feature of the
experience of being in love, and the plot of the play gives a dramatic
heightening to this universal fact by placing this love in the midst of
a feud between the lovers' families, so that it is the development of
the feud, not the characters of the lovers, which destroys them. The
plot itself makes a clear statement about the violent discrepancy between lovers and the world about them; to have individualized Romeo
and Juliet would have blurred the clarity of this statement.

* * *

I have dwelt on the influence of this literary tradition not only to
justify the language of the play but also to indicate where we may
look if we need anything external to tell us where Shakespeare thought
the tragedy of it really lies. In his own sonnets the great theme is that
"every thing that grows/Holds in perfection but a little moment."
"This thought," he said in his sonnets, "is as a death, which cannot
choose/But weep to have that which it fears to lose" (*Sonnets,* 15, 64).
His first really tragic drama is constructed as a series of brief perfec-
tions, each moment perfect because it is the first—until that one of
them which is the last. The play needs no insight, in order to make it
tragic, deeper than this, its chief insight; one so important to Shakespeare that it spills over into *A Midsummer Night's Dream,* where
Lysander says that true love, exposed always to difference of blood,
to war, death and sickness, is

> Swift as a shadow, short as any dream;
> Brief as the lightning in the collied night,

(we remember Juliet's "Too like the lightning, which doth cease to be/
Ere one can say 'It lightens' ")—

> That, in a spleen, unfolds both heaven and earth,
> And ere a man hath power to say "Behold!"
> The jaws of darkness do devour it up:
> So quick bright things come to confusion.   (I. i. 144ff.)

To this Hermione replies, ". . . it is a customary cross." It is, in short,
a tragic aspect of the general human lot. It is no small part of the
greatness of Shakespeare's first real tragedy, as of his later ones, that

the tragedy lies essentially in the condition of man, not of particular men.

T. S. Eliot

. . . We can never emulate music, because to arrive at the condition of music would be the annihilation of poetry, and especially of dramatic poetry. Nevertheless, I have before my eyes a kind of mirage of the perfection of verse drama, which would be a design of human action and of words, such as to present at once the two aspects of dramatic and of musical order. It seems to me that Shakespeare achieved this at least in certain scenes—even rather early, for there is the balcony scene of *Romeo and Juliet*—and that this was what he was striving towards in his late plays. To go as far in this direction as it is possible to go, without losing that contact with the ordinary everyday world with which drama must come to terms, seems to me the proper aim of dramatic poetry. For it is ultimately the function of art, in imposing a credible order upon ordinary reality, and thereby eliciting some perception of an order *in* reality, to bring us to a condition of serenity, stillness, and reconciliation; and then leave us, as Virgil left Dante, to proceed toward a region where that guide can avail us no farther.

*   *   *

In Romeo's beginning, there is still some artificiality:

Two of the fairest stars in all the heaven,
Having some business, do intreat her eyes
To twinkle in their spheres till they return.

For it seems unlikely that a man standing below in the garden, even on a very bright moonlight night, would see the eyes of the lady above flashing so brilliantly as to justify such a comparison. Yet one is aware, from the beginning of this scene, that there is a musical pattern coming, as surprising in its kind as that in the early work of Beethoven. The arrangement of voices—Juliet has three single lines, followed by Romeo's three, four and five, followed by her longer speech—is very remarkable. In this pattern, one feels that it is Juliet's voice that

From "Poetry and Drama," in On Poetry and Poets by T. S. Eliot (London: Faber & Faber Ltd., 1957), pp. 87–88. Copyright 1957 by Faber & Faber Ltd. Reprinted by permission of Faber & Faber Ltd. and Farrar, Straus & Giroux, Inc.

has the leading part: to her voice is assigned the dominant phrase of the whole duet:

> My bounty is as boundless as the sea,
> My love as deep: the more I give to thee
> The more I have, for both are infinite.

And to Juliet is given the key-word "lightning," which occurs again in the play, and is significant of the sudden and disastrous power of her passion, when she says

> 'Tis like the lightning, which doth cease to be
> Ere one can say "it lightens."

In this scene, Shakespeare achieves a perfection of verse which, being perfection, neither he nor anyone else could excel—for this particular purpose. The stiffness, the artificiality, the poetic decoration, of his early verse has finally given place to a simplification to the language of natural speech, and this language of conversation again raised to great poetry, and to great poetry which is essentially dramatic: for the scene has a structure of which each line is an essential part.

John Wain

But where *Hamlet* takes us—albeit stumblingly—into purely tragic territory, the psychological premises of *Romeo and Juliet* are those of the early comedies. Characteristically, those comedies concern themselves with the inborn, unargued stupidity of older people and the life-affirming gaiety and resourcefulness of young ones. The lovers thread their way through obstacles set up by middle-aged vanity and impercipience. Parents are stupid and do not know what is best for their children or themselves: that is a *donnée* and does not have to be justified. *Romeo and Juliet* is in essence a comedy that turns out tragically. That is, it begins with the materials for a comedy—the stupid parental generation, the instant attraction of the young lovers, the quick surface life of street fights, masked balls and comic servants. But this material is blighted. Its gaiety and good fortune are drained away by the fact—also a *donnée*—that the lovers are "star-crossed." It is, to that extent, arbitrarily shaped. It is a tragedy because Shakespeare decided to sit down and write a tragedy. It does not build with in-

From The Living World of Shakespeare *by John Wain (New York: St. Martin's Press, 1964), pp. 107–8. Copyright © 1964 by John Wain. Reprinted by permission of the publisher.*

herently tragic materials. Where the comedies celebrate order by moving from disharmony to harmony, this play moves from surface disharmony to an almost achieved surface harmony, before being dashed by a blow from its author's fist into fundamental, irremediable disaster.

To put it another way, the form of *Romeo and Juliet* is that of a shattered minuet. The two lovers first come together in a dance (Act I, Scene v), and it is noteworthy that the first words they address to each other are in the form of a sonnet. A dance; a sonnet; these are symbols of a formal, contained wholeness. This wholeness is already threatened. Tybalt has recognized Romeo; and though his demand for instant combat has been restrained by his host (a rare case of the older generation's being wiser than the younger), he is glowering and planning revenge. The worm is already in the fruit. But the nature of the worm is not explored. The characters move in a certain pattern because the author has decided on that pattern. Romeo and Juliet are all ardour and constancy, their families are all hatred and pride; no one's motives are mixed, and there are no question marks. After the tragedy the survivors are shocked into dropping their vendetta, and Montague and Capulet are united in grief. Once again, there are no question marks. Nothing made them enemies except the clash of their own wills, and nothing is needed to make them brothers except a change of heart.

E. C. Pettet

Now there are two clear-cut and opposing attitudes to this character [Friar Lawrence]. The first, an emphatically moral one, was satisfactorily stated by Gervinus.

> By Friar Lawrence who, as it were, represents the part of the chorus in this tragedy, the leading idea of the piece is expressed in all fulness . . . that excess in any enjoyment, however pure in itself, transforms its sweet into bitterness, that devotion to any single feeling, however noble, bespeaks its ascendancy; that this ascendancy moves the man and woman out of their natural spheres; that love can only be a companion in life, and cannot fill out the life and business of the man especially.[1]

From "Shakespeare's Detachment from Romance," in Shakespeare and the Romance Tradition *by E. C. Pettet (London: Staples Press Ltd., 1949), pp. 118–21. Reprinted by permission of the publisher.*

[1] Quoted in the Introduction to the Arden *Romeo and Juliet* [London: Methuen & Co. Ltd., 1900, 1917], p. xxxii.

Edward Dowden, on the other hand, would have nothing of these "well-meant moralisings" of Gervinus. He flatly denied that Friar Lawrence is a chorus to the tragedy and regarded him as a type of interfering, middle-aged prudence—something of a milder, more gracious Polonius in fact. "The amiable critic of life as seen from the cloister does not understand life or hate or love; he is not the chorus of the tragedy, but an actor whose wisdom is of a kind which may easily lead himself and others astray." [2]

There is undoubtedly considerable force in these objections of Dowden. For instance, he is obviously right in insisting on the importance of Friar Lawrence as an actor in the drama and on the disastrous outcome of his hopeful attempt to reconcile the Capulet and Montague families. Again, as we have already said, it is a gross distortion of the play to turn it into some sort of moral drama and to argue that any ethical or philosophical idea embodied in Friar Lawrence is the "leading idea of the piece." But a character, active in the drama to some extent, may have a choric function without fulfilling the role of chorus in the formal Greek sense of the word—Horatio is such a character; and characters like Speed, Enobarbus, Thersites may perform a choric function without voicing Shakespeare's simple or settled convictions.

The central idea of Friar Lawrence's long soliloquy is definite enough and fairly expressed by Gervinus' paraphrase: that any single good, pursued blindly in isolation and to extremes, is dangerous and may, by a dialectical process, give rise to its opposite; that every virtue (including love by implication) has its particular good, but no more:

> For nought so vile that on the earth doth live
> But to the earth some special good doth give,
> Nor aught so good but strained from that fair use
> Revolts from true birth, stumbling on abuse:
> Virtue itself turns vice, being misapplied;
> And vice sometimes by action dignified.[3]

This same idea, it should be noticed, is repeated by Friar Lawrence, with an explicit reference to love, just before the marriage of Romeo and Juliet:

> These violent delights have violent ends
> And in their triumph die, like fire and powder,

[2] Introduction, Arden *Romeo and Juliet*, p. xxxiii.
[3] *Romeo and Juliet*, II. iii. 17–22.

Which as they kiss consume: the sweetest honey
Is loathsome in its own deliciousness
And in the taste confounds the appetite.[4]

Of course, this soliloquy of Friar Lawrence is to a large extent simply a piece of dramatic artifice: it bridges the awkward interval between Romeo's exit at the end of the previous scene and his appearance in this, while its references to "baleful weeds and precious-juiced flowers" prepare us for some necessary business of the play that is to follow. But why the length of the soliloquy, why its grave, sincere accent (which is not to be compared with the platitudinous moralisings of Polonius in his "Give thy thoughts no tongue" speech[5]) unless Shakespeare intended it as a significant comment—and a critical one—on the extravagance of the romantic ideal?

But there is no need to leave this objection to Dowden's analysis in mid-air, suspended on an interrogation mark. A few scenes later, in the main current of the play, the attitudes of Romeo and Friar Lawrence are brought into direct conflict, and there can be no doubt which is presented to us in the more favourable light. We cannot, assuredly, be quite unsympathetic to Romeo's retort to the Friar's well-meaning words of comfort and wisdom when he is informed of his banishment:

Heaven is here,
Where Juliet lives; and every cat and dog
And little mouse, every unworthy thing,
Live here in heaven and may look on her;
But Romeo may not.[6]

Philosophy may, as the Friar states, be adversity's sweet milk; our minds allow the proposition. But who ever drank that milk at the right time, in actual and felt adversity? It is the old, old story—the philosopher vainly attempting to assuage a grief he has never, and can never, feel himself; and part of us, rebellious always against the woes of life, applauds when Romeo cries out impatiently:

Hang up philosophy!
Unless philosophy can make a Juliet,
Displant a town, reverse a prince's doom,
It helps not, it prevails not: talk no more.[7]

[4] Ibid., II. vi. 9–13.
[5] Hamlet, I. iii. 59–80.
[6] Romeo and Juliet, III. iii. 29–33.
[7] Ibid., III. iii. 57–60.

This is the moment when we are inclined to agree with Dowden's dismissal of Friar Lawrence as an "amiable critic of life seen from the cloister" who "does not understand life or hate or love." Yet all this is merely a transient reaction. Our total impression of the scene is of an extravagant, pitiful, even ludicrous Romeo reduced to a state of emotional deliquescence like Troilus at the opening of *Troilus and Cressida*. He blubbers, he rolls on the ground, he is hopeless and incapable of stirring a finger to help himself. And this is not the Romeo of the first act—pitiful and absurd in a different, a more callow way —but the grand romantic lover of the Balcony scene and, in a few hours, of the great dawn-farewell to Juliet. The Friar, on the other hand, is altogether admirable: he rises to and dominates the situation. His reproof of Romeo's unmanly despair and desperation, besides pulling Romeo together with the right sort of appeal, is entirely just, and without wasting words he maps out a practical and hopeful course of action for the lovers. By word and deed he completely refutes Dowden's interpretation of him, and Romeo, as always, except when he is grief-distraught, appreciates his sterling worth:

> But that a joy past calls out on me,
> It were a grief, so brief to part with thee.[8]

The sorry spectacle that Romeo, the romantic lover, makes of himself in this scene should not be regarded in isolation, for it points directly forward to the catastrophe. Admittedly, he does not bear the responsibility for that catastrophe that Othello and Anthony bear for the disasters in which they are overwhelmed. But if the efficient cause of the catastrophe in *Romeo and Juliet* is an accident, this catastrophe is hastened by Romeo himself who, when he hears the false report of Juliet's death, reveals the same weaknesses that he had shown when Friar Lawrence had informed him of his banishment—reckless impulsiveness, an incapacity to think, and a despair that turns instantly to thoughts of suicide. But this time there is no Friar Lawrence to stand beside him, and he perishes miserably.

Bertrand Evans

More than any other of Shakespeare's—even more than *Othello*, as a count of pertinent data shows—*Romeo and Juliet* is a tragedy of

---

From "*The Brevity of Friar Laurence*" by Bertrand Evans, in PMLA, LXV (*1950*), 850–52. Copyright 1950 by the Modern Language Association of America. Reprinted by permission of the publisher.

[8] *Romeo and Juliet*, III. iii. 173–174.

unawareness. Fate, or Heaven, as the Prince calls it, or the "greater power," as the Friar calls it, working out its purpose without the use of either a human villain or a supernatural agent sent to intervene in mortal affairs, operates through the common human condition of not knowing. Participants in the action, some of them in parts that are minor and seem insignificant, contribute one by one the indispensable stitches which make the pattern, and contribute them not knowing; that is to say, they act when they do not know the truth of the situation in which they act, this truth being known, however, to us who are spectators. All these persons might cry at last, with Claudio of *Much Ado about Nothing*, "O, what men dare do! what men may do! What men daily do, not knowing what they do" (IV, i, 19–21). Even after the Friar has spoken all that he knows to speak, however, most of them have learned not even enough to pass this judgment, for the visions of only a few are ever widened enough for them to see the significance of their own past actions. In the line of true descent, which is in fact the *way* Fate worked, neither Romeo's "wild-eyed fury" nor the accidental detention of Friar John looms so large as the positive actions of those who do what they do in moments of ignorance of the situation which then exists. It is these actions, I believe, that we must re-examine to expose the pattern of the tragedy.

Although the feud named in the Prologue has long existed, the tragic pattern with which we are concerned as spectators is shown to begin in the first scene of the play.

* * *

. . . This initial action is of a kind with actions which follow, through which are made the essential contributions to the tragic outcome. The unawareness of the servants here differs in degree, rather than in kind, from the unawareness of situation in which later Capulet, for example, acts. The difference is that when this initial action takes place no fully developed situation as yet exists, whereas in Capulet's later moments of decision and action a fully developed situation does exist, of which Capulet is unaware. However, we know that an enveloping situation exists when the servants act, for we heard in Shakespeare's Prologue a clear warning that what immediately follows will exhibit Fate at work. Sampson and Gregory, Abram and Balthasar intend no injury to the children of their respective masters. When they act, they cannot possibly guess the consequences of their actions. Furthermore, they cannot and do not ever know either how they contributed or *that* they contributed to the final catastrophe. If they are present in the last scene of the play—and certainly they should be present among the citizens who view the spectacle and wonder how it came to be—they cannot connect any act of theirs with this end. When the time has come to view the bodies in the tomb, the pattern, as we have already seen, has been obscured by its own darkness, and the participants can only gape as Friar Laurence, himself shaken by the knowledge of his unawareness, diffuses just light enough to enable recognition, among the survivors, of the most obvious means. The many particular acts, inconspicuous as they seemed trivial to the actors, though in fact indispensable in the full pattern, are gone and irrecoverable.

Nevill Coghill

. . . let us watch his pictorial imagination at work upon a known source and see how it is transformed so as to make visible and to intensify the meaning of the action narrated. The undisputed source of *Romeo and Juliet* is Arthur Brooke's *Tragicall Historye of Romeus and Juliet,* published in 1562. Two examples of the Shakespearean transformation will be enough to make our point.

Brooke's poem begins with a topographical description of Verona:[1]

> Bylt in an happy time, bylt on a fertile soyle,
> Maynteined by the heavenly fates, and by the townish toyle.
> The fruitfull hilles above, the pleasant vales belowe,
> The silver streame with channell depe, that through the towne doth
>   flow, *etc.*   (3–6)

and so we come to an equally general account of the uneasy situation between the Capelets and the Montagews.

> A wonted use it is, that men of likely sorte
> (I wot not by what furye forsd) envye eche others porte.
> So these, whose egall state bred envye pale of hew,
> And then of grudging envyes roote, blacke hate and rancor grewe.

From Shakespeare's Professional Skills *by Nevill Coghill (Cambridge, England: The University Press, 1964), pp. 28–31. Copyright © 1964 by Cambridge University Press. Reprinted by permission of the publisher.*

[1] Quotations from Shakespeare's sources are taken from Professor Geoffrey Bullough's edition of them, in five volumes, entitled *Narrative and Dramatic Sources of Shakespeare* (London and New York, 1957), unless otherwise stated.

As of a little sparke, oft ryseth mighty fyre,
So of a kyndled sparke of grudge, in flames flash out theyr yre,
And then theyr deadly foode, first hatchd of trifling stryfe
Did bathe in bloud of smarting woundes, it re[a]ved breth and lyfe.
No legend lye I tell, scarce yet theyr eyes be drye
That did behold the grisly sight, with wet and weping eye.
But when the prudent prince, who there the scepter helde,
So great a new disorder in his common weale behelde
By jentyl meane he sought, their choler to asswage,
And by perswasion to appease, their blameful furious rage.
But both his woords and tyme, the prince hath spent in vayne
So rooted was the inward hate, he lost his buysy payne.   (31–46)

This generalised narration has little for a reader's inward eye: there
are grudging envies and black hates, but no men: there is the blood
of smarting wounds and the wet of weeping eyes, but no particular
fight: there is a persuasive prince but we do not see him at work.

But with Shakespeare and the stage, all that is general becomes
particular, all that is abstract becomes human: the feud between the
rival houses flames out in a specific and visible brawl, into which
Tybalt hurls himself (we do not hear of Tybalt in Brooke until nearly
a thousand lines later in the story). In short, the play begins with a
violent picture of a faction fight fanned up out of nothing in which
every detail is sharply visualised:

Offi. Clubs, Bils, and Partisons, strike, beat them down
          Downe with the *Capulets,* downe with the *Mountagues.*
               Enter old Capulet in his Gowne and his wife.
Cap. What a noise is this? Giue me my long Sword ho.
Wife. A crutch, a crutch: why call you for a Sword?
Cap. My Sword I say: Old *Mountague* is come,
          And flourishes his Blade in spight of me.   (I, i, 70–6)

This is the dialogue of a man with eyes, and who can make images
that work instantly upon a stage for other eyes. It was a talent of his
to start his plays with something visually stunning, the image of an
idea.

But a more striking example than that which shows us the enmity
of Capulet and Montague in being is that which shows us Romeo
and Juliet falling in love. Arthur Brooke describes the scene with
embarrassing ineptitude at considerable length. When he reaches the
point, we are offered the preposterous picture of Juliet seated, with

Mercutio gripping her right hand, and Romeo her left hand; Mercutio began it:

> With friendly gripe he ceasd * fayre Juliet's snowish hand . . .
> As soone as had the knight the vyrgins right hand raught
> Within his trembling hand her left hath loving Romeus caught . . .
> Then she with tender hand his tender palme hath prest,
> What joy trow you was graffed so in Romeus cloven brest?   (259–68)

This absurd group of three hand-holders is nothing to Shakespeare's purpose, and shows nothing of the forces that empower the tragedy. At Shakespeare's dance, music plays—for on a stage we can have music —and we see the bumbling *empressement* of Capulet's hospitality: next we are aware of Romeo:

> What Ladie is that which doth inrich the hand
> Of yonder Knight?
> *Ser.* I know not sir.
> *Rom.* O she doth teach the Torches to burne bright, *etc.*   (I, iv. 39–41)

and his soliloquy is his declaration of love over the background of the music and the dancing: but it is overheard by Tybalt, and his rage, hardly governed by Old Capulet, brings back the dangers of the opening street-brawl and remakes the image of hatred from the midst of which, at this instant, love is to spring: for as Tybalt storms angrily out, the dance has brought Juliet to where Romeo is standing, which, since he has just been in soliloquy, I take to be down-stage, out on the apron.

And now they are together, and they kiss: and their kiss is so important to them that they weave a sonnet round it, and are almost into a sonnet-sequence, when the Nurse interrupts them. A kiss is the visual image of love, the simplest, the oldest, the most beautiful, the easiest symbol in the art of theatre: here, at the beginning of the story, we see this kiss, instantly following upon Tybalt's rage, juxtaposed images of the two great passions that power the play, and which in the end destroy one another. It is a meaning that can be *seen*.

* Read "seized."

Chronology of Important Dates

Dates for plays are approximate, and indicate first performances.

Shakespeare	The Age
1558	Beginning of Queen Elizabeth's reign.
1562	Arthur Brooke's poem, *The Tragicall Historye of Romeus and Juliet.*
1564 Shakespeare born at Stratford-upon-Avon; baptized April 26.	
1576	Opening of the first permanent playhouse in England, The Theatre.
1582 Marriage to Anne Hathaway.	
1584–88	John Lyly's romantic love comedies.
1587	Thomas Kyd's *The Spanish Tragedy*; Christopher Marlowe's *Tamburlaine*; Brooke's *Romeus* reissued.
1588	Defeat of the Spanish Armada.
1591–93 The three *Henry VI* plays; *Richard III; Titus Andronicus; Comedy of Errors; Taming of the Shrew*; first printed reference to Shakespeare in London by Robert Greene.	Sir Philip Sidney's sonnet sequence, *Astrophel and Stella* (1591); Marlowe's *Doctor Faustus* and *Edward II*; sonnet cycles by Samuel Daniel, Henry Constable, and many others.
1593 *Venus and Adonis*, Shakespeare's first published work.	

1594	*The Rape of Lucrece.*	Lord Chamberlain's Company of actors formed with Shakespeare as a sharer.
1594–96	*Two Gentlemen of Verona; Love's Labour's Lost; King John; Richard II; Romeo and Juliet; Midsummer Night's Dream.*	Edmund Spenser's sonnet cycle, the *Amoretti* (1595).
1597–99	*Merchant of Venice;* the two parts of *Henry IV; Henry V; Much Ado about Nothing; Julius Caesar; As You Like It; Twelfth Night.*	Opening of the Globe playhouse (1599).
1600–1603	*Merry Wives of Windsor; Hamlet; Troilus and Cressida; All's Well That Ends Well.*	Rebellion of the Earl of Essex (1601).
1603		Death of Queen Elizabeth; accession of James I; Lord Chamberlain's Company becomes The King's Men.
1604–6	*Measure for Measure; Othello; King Lear; Macbeth.*	The Gunpowder Plot (1605). Ben Jonson's *Volpone* (1606).
1607–9	*Antony and Cleopatra; Timon of Athens; Coriolanus; Pericles; Cymbeline;* publication of the *Sonnets.*	The King's Men acquire the Blackfriars Playhouse (1609).
1610–11	*The Winter's Tale; The Tempest.*	Jonson's *The Alchemist* (1610). The King James Bible (1611).
1612	Retirement to Stratford-upon-Avon.	John Webster's *The White Devil.*
1616	Shakespeare's death, April 23.	Jonson's *Works* published in Folio.
1623	The First Folio edition of Shakespeare's plays.	

Notes on the Editor and Contributors

DOUGLAS COLE, editor of this volume, is Professor of English at Northwestern University. He is the author of *Suffering and Evil in the Plays of Christopher Marlowe* and of several essays on Elizabethan and modern drama.

H. B. CHARLTON (1890–1961) was Professor of English at the University of Manchester. His *Shakespearian Comedy* is a companion volume to his work on tragedy.

W. H. CLEMEN, Professor of English at the University of Munich, has taught as a visitor in both England and the United States. His distinguished scholarship in medieval and Elizabethan literature includes *English Tragedy Before Shakespeare* and *Shakespeare's Soliloquies*.

NEVILL COGHILL was Merton Professor of English Literature at Oxford, 1957–1966. Long a Fellow and Tutor of Exeter College, his reputation as a medievalist and translator of Chaucer was matched by his practical skills as director and producer of dramatics at Oxford for over thirty years.

FRANKLIN M. DICKEY teaches Renaissance literature at the University of New Mexico, where he is Professor of English.

T. S. ELIOT (1888–1965), the renowned poet and critic, was also a Director of Faber & Faber, Ltd. in London. His literary studies include *The Sacred Wood, Elizabethan Essays,* and *Poetry and Drama.*

BERTRAND EVANS, Professor of English at the University of California at Berkeley, is the author of *Shakespeare's Comedies.*

HARLEY GRANVILLE-BARKER (1877–1946), actor, playwright, producer, and lecturer, was one of the English theater's most prominent twentieth-century figures. Besides his *Prefaces to Shakespeare* he also wrote *The Use of the Drama, On Dramatic Method,* and (with G. B. Harrison) *A Companion to Shakespeare Studies.*

HARRY LEVIN, Irving Babbitt Professor of Comparative Literature at Harvard University, is the author of *The Overreacher: A Study of Christopher Marlowe* and *The Question of Hamlet.*

WINIFRED NOWOTTNY is Senior Lecturer in English at University College, University of London, and author of *The Language Poets Use*.

E. C. PETTET teaches English literature at Goldsmiths' College in the University of London. Besides his work on Shakespeare, he has written books on the poetry of Vaughan and Keats.

CAROLINE F. E. SPURGEON (1869–1942) was a pioneer in the imagery analysis of Shakespeare's plays. She wrote extensively on many aspects of English literature, and was Professor of English at the University of London.

ELMER EDGAR STOLL (1874–1959) was Professor of English at the University of Minnesota, and one of America's foremost interpreters of Shakespeare, stressing Renaissance backgrounds of thought and dramatic convention. His many books include *Art and Artifice in Shakespeare* and *Shakespeare Studies*.

JAMES SUTHERLAND, a distinguished scholar of eighteenth-century literature, has also edited several Shakespearean plays. From 1951 to 1967 he was Lord Northcliffe Professor at the University of London.

JOHN WAIN was Lecturer in English Literature at the University of Reading before becoming a free lance critic and author of fiction and poetry. His criticism includes *Essays on Literature and Ideas*.

JOHN DOVER WILSON, formerly Regius Professor of Rhetoric and English Literature at the University of Edinburgh, is an accomplished and controversial editor and critic of Shakespeare's plays. He has written *Life in Shakespeare's England, The Fortunes of Falstaff,* and *What Happens in Hamlet*.

Selected Bibliography

Bonnard, Georges A., *"Romeo and Juliet:* A Possible Significance?" *Review of English Studies,* New Series Vol. II (1951), 319–27. An examination of Shakespeare's alterations of source material for tragic effects.

Goddard, Harold C., *The Meaning of Shakespeare.* Chicago: University of Chicago Press, 1951. The chapter on *Romeo and Juliet* focuses on the moral stature of the chief characters.

Lawlor, John, *"Romeo and Juliet," Early Shakespeare,* ed. by John R. Brown and Bernard Harris, *Stratford-upon-Avon Studies 3.* London: Edward Arnold (Publishers) Ltd., 1961, pp. 123–43. Relates the play to medieval conceptions of tragedy and to Shakespeare's other tragedies.

Mahood, M. M., *Shakespeare's Wordplay.* London: Methuen & Co. Ltd., 1957. Besides discussing wordplay, the author argues well against the view which sees the play as a version of the *Liebestod* myth.

Ribner, Irving, *Patterns in Shakespearian Tragedy.* London: Methuen & Co. Ltd., 1960. Sees the play and its hero in terms of Senecan stoicism.

Siegel, Paul N., "Christianity and the Religion of Love in *Romeo and Juliet," Shakespeare Quarterly,* XII (1961), 371–92. Compares Shakespeare's treatment of the lovers with that found in the play's sources and analogues.

Stauffer, Donald A., *Shakespeare's World of Images.* New York: W. W. Norton & Co., Inc., 1949. Contains a succinct and balanced analysis of the play's imagery and themes.

Stirling, Brents, *Unity in Shakespearean Tragedy.* New York: Columbia University Press, 1956. The chapter on *Romeo and Juliet* analyzes the play's theme of haste.

TWENTIETH CENTURY
INTERPRETATIONS

MAYNARD MACK, *Series Editor*
Yale University

NOW AVAILABLE
Collections of Critical Essays
ON

(continued on next page)

(*continued from previous page*)

HENRY IV, PART TWO
HENRY V
THE ICEMAN COMETH
JULIUS CAESAR
KEATS'S ODES
LIGHT IN AUGUST
LORD JIM
MUCH ADO ABOUT NOTHING
THE NIGGER OF THE "NARCISSUS"
OEDIPUS REX
THE OLD MAN AND THE SEA
PAMELA
THE PLAYBOY OF THE WESTERN WORLD
THE PORTRAIT OF A LADY
A PORTRAIT OF THE ARTIST AS A YOUNG MAN
THE PRAISE OF FOLLY
PRIDE AND PREJUDICE
THE RAPE OF THE LOCK
THE RIME OF THE ANCIENT MARINER
ROBINSON CRUSOE
ROMEO AND JULIET
SAMSON AGONISTES
THE SCARLET LETTER
SIR GAWAIN AND THE GREEN KNIGHT
SONGS OF INNOCENCE AND OF EXPERIENCE
THE SOUND AND THE FURY
THE TEMPEST
TESS OF THE D'URBERVILLES
TOM JONES
TWELFTH NIGHT
UTOPIA
VANITY FAIR
WALDEN
THE WASTE LAND
WOMEN IN LOVE
WUTHERING HEIGHTS